GHOST OF
THE HARDY BOYS

Ghost of
THE HARDY BOYS

An Autobiography by
LESLIE McFARLANE

METHUEN / Two Continents
Toronto • New York • London • Sydney • Wellington

ISBN Canada 0-458-91410-X

ISBN U.S.A. 0-8467-0157-X

Library of Congress
Catalog Card Number 75-39095

Cover design by Alan Daniel

Cataloguing in Publication Data

McFarlane, Leslie, 1902-
    Ghost of the Hardy boys

ISBN 0-458-91410-X (Toronto).
ISBN 0-8467-0157-X (New York).

1. McFarlane, Leslie, 1902-   2. Dixon,
Franklin W. The Hardy boys mystery stories.
I. Title.

PS8524.F35Z5   C813.'5'2   C76-017001-0
PR9199.3.M25Z5

Published in the United States by
Methuen/Two Continents Publications
30 East 42 St., New York 10017

Printed and bound
in the United States of America

1 2 3 4 5   0 9 8 7 6

To Patricia, Norah and Brian,
who grew up with the boys

Contents

Introduction

It has been nearly fifty years since I hammered out the first Hardy Boys' escapade on my secondhand Underwood in a cabin in northern Ontario.

Frank and Joe Hardy came into the world on motorcycles, speeding down a road by the ocean on a sunny morning in Spring. As they sped, they engaged in dialogue.

Don't ask how they managed this with two motorcycles going full blast. They just did.

> *"After the help we gave Dad on that forgery case, I guess he'll begin to think we could be detectives when we grow up."*
>
> *"Why shouldn't we? Isn't he one of the most famous detectives in the country? And aren't we his sons? If the profession was good enough for him to follow it should be good enough for us."*
>
> *Two bright-eyed boys on motorcycles were speeding along a shore road....*

Very neat. In less than seventy-five words we knew where we were.

Now to identify the lads and establish them *"near their home town of Bayport, a city of 50,000 inhabitants, located on Barmet Bay on the Atlantic coast."*

Don't bother to look it up. You won't find it on the map.

The road is narrow. A steep wall of rock rises sharply on the left. On the right a precipitous cliff drops straight down to the hungry sea below.

Suddenly, around a curve, a car appears.

Out of control, driven at reckless speed by some red-headed maniac who should never have been given a license, skidding and swerving, the car hurtles toward the boys on their motorcycles.

"He'll run us down!" shouts Joe, in alarm.

At this point, I, in my new role of Franklin W. Dixon, stared at the typewriter for a while, considered the situation, and wrote: "Indeed, the position of the two boys was perilous."

From this beginning, a great industry was born.

GHOST OF
THE HARDY BOYS

CHAPTER 1:

Fiction Writer Wanted

In the Springtime of 1926 I found Springfield, Massachusetts, a delightful place. I was twenty-three, healthy and footloose, free to latch onto any opportunity, pick up any challenge. The ad that ran in the classified columns of the trade journal *Editor and Publisher* seemed to combine both.

Experienced Fiction Writer Wanted
to Work from
Publisher's Outlines

A box number was appended for replies. That was all. Because most of the other ads were for reporters, deskmen and copy-writers this one stood out. Who ever heard of anyone actually advertising for the services of a fiction writer?

I considered my experience, which didn't take long. *Adventure*, a popular magazine founded on the shaky policy that its fiction should ignore women, had published some of my stories. True, they weren't very good stories and the magazine had bounced back several recent submissions in rapid succession, but who was asking? Experience I could claim.

So I sat down at my typewriter in the cityroom of the *Springfield Republican*, hammered out a reply to the ad and dropped it in the mailbox. Then I went about my business, which was to cover the hotel beat for the day and work up some kind of feature piece that might give a little sparkle to the Sunday edition.

Earlier that year, flat broke and out of work, I had arrived for an interview at the *Republican* office with twenty cents in my pocket. Bill Walsh, a gentle man who looked pretty young to have given up the fight against baldness, was not exactly awed when I was ushered to his desk. I have never been an imposing figure but in that year of grace I was five foot three, 105 pounds, and no one could have looked less like a swashbuckling newshound.

After informing him that I was a Canadian, born in the Ottawa Valley, brought up in a northern Ontario mining camp and that I didn't get past high school, I showed him a dozen news clippings with my byline and told him of my employment record in the newspaper world. First, a job as reporter on the *Cobalt Daily Nugget.* . . .

"Where is Cobalt?" Mr. Walsh inquired gently.

"Northern Ontario. The biggest silver stampede in history was at Cobalt."

"That must have been exciting."

"It was over by the time I got there. Then I worked several years on the *Sudbury Star* . . . ."

"Sudbury?"

"Northern Ontario again. The world's biggest nickel mine is at Sudbury. After that I worked for a while on the *Ottawa Journal*, then the *Montreal Herald*. I have also written a lot of stuff for magazines."

I thought his face clouded a little, so I showed him a few battered copies of *Adventure* with some of my stories in print. The magazine fiction suggested that I wasn't a newspaperman at heart, merely a freelance fiction writer toughing out a bad run of rejections. This, in fact, was true. However, he not only hired me at forty dollars a week, but handed over an advance of twenty dollars against the first week's pay.

The cash advance he regarded as an occupational hazard. There had been occasions when the kindness of Mr. Walsh was betrayed by itinerants who departed to celebrate their prosperity in the nearest speakeasy, never to be seen again on *Republican* premises. But even these lessons failed to harden his heart the next time he signed on another busted journeyman with a batch of clippings and a hungry look. All journeyman reporters were alike he later told me. They invariably showed up in a battered hat and a disreputable raincoat with the familiar green *American Mercury* sticking precariously out of one pocket, broke and looking hungover or hungry. Once, he confessed, a candidate had shown up without a copy of the *Mercury* and although Walsh hired the man it was against his better judgment. He had an instinctive feeling that the fellow was a fraud, which, of course, he was.

I left the *Republican* in high spirits; I had a job *and* twenty dollars. Most of the money evaporated quickly, some in a nearby diner, some as payment for a week's rent in a Pearl Street rooming house. When I interviewed my landlord, Mr. Arbuthnot, I was glad my strength had been fortified with a meal. A peppery old gent with a bristling mustache, he made it clear that the shelter of his roof was not available to every Tom, Dick and Harry who came along.

"You a boozer?" he barked.

"No sir."

"Catch you with booze in your room, out you go. Smoke?"

"Well...yes."

"Filthy habit. Ruins your system. Softens the brain. You a godly boy?"

"Godly?"

"You been saved?"

I was tempted to tell Mr. Arbuthnot that I had just been saved by Bill Walsh's advance on salary, then decided he might regard it as flippant. Instead, I applauded the moral standards of this cheerless codger and told him my trunk and typewriter would arrive in the morning. On the bedside table I found a selection of tracts, most of them suggesting that Armageddon was just around the corner. They all quoted extensively from the Book of Revelations and were calculated to inspire nightmares about zoological freaks with eight or nine heads.

In 1926, Springfield, Massachusetts, was a very pleasant city and I have no doubt it is a very pleasant city today, although I have never been back to find out. But even civic boosters would have to admit that it has never been the kind of city that consistently gives birth to Big News and huge black headlines in the national press. If there was anything distinctive about the *Republican* it was that its fame had been founded not on news but on editorials. Even in 1926 there were men in the *Republican* office who spoke fondly of the great days when the paper was known as the voice of the Republican party and the editorials of the late, great Samuel Bowles were read with respect and quoted widely, with power to devastate and to elevate. It was even said that there had been a time when bright, young New England university graduates, if they came from approved families, would be allowed to pay for the privilege of working as *Republican* reporters. The paper was regarded as a great school of journalism. If you could meet the *Republican* standards you could work anywhere. Those days were long gone when I arrived. Nevertheless, one soon learned that newspapermen on the *Republican* had a sense of pride in their paper and standards to uphold.

I was assigned to the "hotel beat" which really wasn't a beat at all because there was only one big hotel. When a celebrity blew into town, usually on a lecture tour, he always checked in at the Hotel Kimball and made it known that he was not averse to being interviewed. Kindly Bill Walsh gave me this beat because he thought I could do with a little fattening up. All major banquets were held at the Kimball. The place was booked solidly for service club luncheons. Every noonday was good for a service club meal on the cuff and one could always count on a couple of lavish dinners—usually political in origin—every week.

It didn't take long to see that nothing much ever happened in Springfield, Massachusetts. The *Republican*, which was a morning paper, had one rival, the *Union*, which hit the streets every afternoon. If anything newsworthy happened before five p.m., they covered it; after five, we covered it. Every day the deskmen scalped the columns of the rival paper and ordered rewrites.

In the movies, reporters were always pictured as competing ferociously with one another for "scoops," but in Springfield we viewed that approach as film fiction nonsense. Any reporter green enough to come dashing in, all excited and in a lather, claiming a big scoop, would have been rewarded with sour looks. Then an old hand would have taken him aside and explained firmly that, in our town, scoops were not encouraged.

He who liveth by the scoop, he would be advised, often dieth by the scoop. The two newspapers had their own public and weren't all that competitive. Live and let live was the philosophy.

Under such easygoing conditions it might be assumed that every reporter was content. Not so. Just about everyone aspired to improve his lot.

Buddy Brooks, the Churches and Obits man, wrote songs on the side. He had even achieved publication and gave us all copies of a lachrymose number called "That Dear Old Mother of Mine" to prove it. We suspected that he paid the printer's bill himself.

Creaver, the City Hall man, was stagestruck. He performed in amateur plays all over town and when a big production visited locally, he could always count on a job as an extra at the State. Inevitably, he hoped, he would be "discovered." Merit cannot remain hidden forever.

Jacobsen, the police reporter, a dour fellow who was said to have found cheap lodgings in a bawdy house to lend an air of respectability to the place, made no secret of the fact that he was writing a novel. Just about everyone on the staff harbored this ambition, but Jacobsen was the only one who had reached Chapter Two. He read passages to us from time to time. Gloomy stuff, it sounded a lot like Dreiser, with shorter sentences and longer words.

As for me, I was writing a play.

During the previous year *Adventure* had printed one of my more ambitious tales, 20,000 words long, called "Impostor," about a broken-down fur trader who presided over a broken-down trading post in the Hudson Bay wilderness. Because I was living in northern Ontario when this manuscript went into the mail, the editors of *Adventure* assumed that I had a profound knowledge of wilderness life—indeed, that I might even be a broken-down fur trader myself. So they published the story.

Alan Dinehart, a popular actor of the day, read it in Chicago while touring in a comedy called *Applesauce*. Not only did he like it but he decided that a drama of the north woods might be just what he needed for a change of pace . Not that he wanted to stumble around the stage in a role of a drink-sodden reprobate. That wasn't his bag. Mr. Dinehart, who was blessed with an ingratiating personality, liked the part of the upstanding young adventurer who arrived at the trading post posing as the factor's grandson.

He sent off a telegram to *Adventure* offering to buy the rights for $500. When this was conveyed to me I rejected it promptly. Everyone knew that playwrights earned huge sums of money on Broadway and always ended up in Hollywood owning mansions and mistresses. I was not interested in paltry sums. I would write the play myself, so eventually we got together to discuss turning "Impostor" into a starring vehicle for Mr. Dinehart.

Two little matters bothered him, he confessed. First, I had never written a play. Second, the story — like most *Adventure* stories — lacked female characters. It would be necessary, he thought, to introduce an attractive young woman with whom the imposter, played by Dinehart, would fall in love. His public would expect it.

The great thing about reaching the age of twenty-three is that nothing seems impossible. I assured Dinehart that if my lack of experience in dramaturgy disturbed him, he need have no fears. I was quite positive that I could come up with two and a half hours of lively dialogue and tense action. As for female interest I could see no reason why a luscious damsel could not become involved in the goings-on at the trading post. She could be a missionary's motherless daughter, helping her father bring the word of God to the heathen. In fact I could even supply another girl, if he liked, a fiery halfbreed of jealous disposition and explosive temperament.

Mr. Dinehart was cheered. We shook hands and parted.

Now, confronting my typewriter every morning in my room on Pearl Street, I tried to bring my confident promises to life. Because reporters weren't required to show up at the *Republican* office before two o'clock in the afternoon, the mornings were free for the daily tussle with the broken-down trader. It became more than a tussle. It became a battle, and a losing battle at that.

There is a great difference, I found, between the creation of a small piece of fiction in which the characters are free to roam all over the place and the construction of a play which confines them to a one-room trading post. The problems become even tougher when this trading post is so far north that it has no phone service.

True, playwrights did get along somehow before Mr. Bell perfected his invention, but only after a fashion. Even Shakespeare must have deplored the necessity of having messengers running in and out of his palaces all the time with letters like player-piano rolls that sometimes took fifteen minutes to read aloud.

The trouble was that the trading post was just too small. My characters kept bumping into each other. One was forever forced to invent plausible reasons for sending them outside or bringing them indoors again when they were needed. To make way for an exchange of confidences between hero and heroine it would be necessary, for example, to get the girl's father off-stage. A playwriting manual picked up at the Springfield Public Library insisted that all exits and entrances had to be motivated. It wouldn't do to let the old man just open the door and walk out, as occasionally happens in everyday life. He had to explain himself. Apparently there was some kind of law that governed these matters. The manual was pretty firm about it.

It called for a lot of hard thinking. The old man might say:

"I must step out and have a word with Chief Snapping Turtle. The pemmican supply is running low."

Shrewd and inventive dialogue.

But the catch was that he couldn't use the same excuse twice. Not unless he returned almost immediately to announce: "Chief Snapping Turtle has gone ptrapping ptarmigan. I'll ptalk to him about the pemmican later." In which event there was no point in sending him out in the first place. And he certainly couldn't say, "I have to go out for a leak," like any normal man.

As for the heroine, the missionary's beautiful daughter, she gave no end of trouble. A latecomer who didn't even exist in the original story, she never seemed quite at home. I could fancy the old fur trader gazing dourly at this stranger and wondering where the hell she came from. And getting her off-stage called for a variety of excuses. I recall three.

"Excuse me, it's time for me to go and milk the moose."

"I hope you folks will pardon me but I must skin a beaver."

"Forgive me but I have to go out back and read the mail-order catalog."

None of them got her halfway through Act One.

I bogged down shortly after the opening of Act Two. It had become clear that the plot needed complication, conflict and suspense—more of everything. The characters needed character. The dialogue needed sense. Reluctantly, I came to the conclusion that the art of dramaturgy was not to be mastered overnight. Not, at least, by me. After a month's work, with all my characters jostling each other in front of the trading post fireplace, I decided to abandon them for a while and wrote Dinehart a note to that effect.

I arrived in the cityroom that day in a chastened frame of mind. It is disconcerting for a young man to admit that there are limits to his abilities. I brightened up when I found a letter in the mailbox. It bore the return address of The Stratemeyer Syndicate, at 519 Main Street, East Orange, New Jersey.

By this time I had almost forgotten the ad in *Editor and Publisher*, answered almost three weeks before. A syndicate in

East Orange didn't sound much like a big publishing house in New York. But this letter was indeed a reply—and it indicated that I had been chosen.

The letter was signed, in crabbed handwriting, "Edward Stratemeyer."

This name meant nothing to me at all.

How was I to know that I was gazing at the signature of the most prolific author of the day, a Henry Ford of fiction for boys and girls?

Yours truly, Edward Stratemeyer.

It didn't mean a thing.

CHAPTER 2:

You, Too, Can Be Roy Rockwood

Edward Stratemeyer's reply gave no hint of his place in the world of letters. It merely stated that my answer to the advertisement in *Editor and Publisher* had been favorably considered and went on to explain that the Stratemeyer Syndicate prepared book manuscripts for publishers, with special emphasis on series designed for juvenile readers.

Mr. Stratemeyer confessed that although he had personally written some of these volumes, the claims upon his time in recent months were such that he had been forced to concentrate on planning new series and plotting new books. The actual writing he now assigned to others.

Most of his writers were professionals. Some of them, he suggested without giving away any secrets, were actually very well known to the reading public. When they wrote for Mr. Stratemeyer, however, their identities were concealed behind "house names" which belonged to the Syndicate.

Under separate cover he was sending me two sample books. Each represented a successful series that might be particularly suited to my talents.

One was from "The Nat Ridley Rapid Fire Detective Stories," a series which had now reached a total of fifteen volumes. Each dealt with the adventures of a clever and daring young detective in his personal war against crime. Although the detective's name was Nat Ridley, he was not to be confused with the author, Nat Ridley, Jr., who wrote in third person. And although Nat Ridley was a detective, and a brainy one, Mr. Stratemeyer cautioned that Nat Ridley, Jr. was not encouraged to dwell at length on his namesake's mental processes. They were apt to slow down a book. When Nat Ridley came up against a mystery, he didn't spend much time thinking his way through its mazes. He just went out and did something about it. A man of action.

The other book, which fell under the heading of "outdoor adventure," was part of "The Dave Fearless Series." Half a dozen of these titles had already been published, narrating the exploits of a young deep-sea diver and underwater explorer named, of course, Dave Fearless.

Mr. Stratemeyer suggested that I read the two specimen books and choose one. Informed of my choice he would then send me an outline of the opening chapters of the series volume presently in preparation, which I would be asked to expand into about 2,000 words of publishable fiction. This trial run would not, of course, involve payment. However, if the two chapters pleased Mr. Stratemeyer, he would commission me to complete the book, twenty chapters in all, for a guaranteed sum of $100, flat rate, no royalty, with the prospect of further lucrative assignments to follow.

The letter opened a window on a very strange corner of the publishing world. It had never occurred to me that books could be written and printed in this odd fashion. But why question the methods of an established author? If Edward Stratemeyer decided that it was quicker and easier to conjure up plots in preference to writing entire books, if he thought it sound policy to hire wordsmiths to turn his plots into publishable manuscripts, who was I to criticize?

A brown-paper parcel on the mail desk yielded the sample volumes. They were paperbacks. Today this generally means that the book has achieved success in hard covers. In 1926 it meant either that it was beneath contempt or that it was a pirated classic at least fifty years old.

The "Nat Ridley Rapid Fire Detective Stories" series

offered a gaudy cover in yellow, red, blue and black which portrayed a jut-jawed young man aiming a pistol at a sinister brute who held aloft a stick of dynamite with sizzling fuse attached. This confrontation was somewhere in the depths of a mine. The jut-jawed youth was apparently unaware of a snarling scamp who had sneaked up behind him, intent on braining him with a sledgehammer. If you wanted to know how it came out you would have to read *Tracked to the West* (or *Nat Ridley at the Magnet Mine*) by Nat Ridley, Jr. And I always thought magnets came from hardware stores.

The other book cover illustrated a tense moment in the lives of two young men and a polar bear who shared an ice floe somewhere in the Arctic Ocean. The floe was so small that obviously the bear or the young men would have to leave. The bear seemed to have made up his mind to stay and was prepared to defend his frigid claim with tooth and claw. The title of this one was *Dave Fearless Among the Icebergs* (or *The Secret of the Eskimo Igloo*) and it was designated as Volume Four of "The Dave Fearless Series." The author's name was given as Roy Rockwood.

Roy Rockwood?

I couldn't believe it.

Roy Rockwood belonged right up there with the immortals. He was the creator of Bomba the Jungle Boy, idol of every red-blooded kid in the Western world.

Bomba the Jungle Boy!

Bomba, the wilderness lad whose adventures in many volumes provided an endless survival course for thousands of youngsters who were never likely to find themselves within miles of a jungle. Bomba, the youth who talked with the wild beasts and made them his friends. Bomba, the resourceful, the greatest tracker, runner, wrestler and climber of them all. Bomba, the kid who made Tarzan look like a copycat.

Edgar Rice Burroughs had his followers no doubt, mainly among the prune juice set. They were welcome to any entertainment they could find in the acrobatics of the aging Tarzan. But Roy Rockwood had his disciples, too, just as devout and a good deal younger; their name was legion, and Bomba was their prophet. What worshipper cared, if he ever knew, that Tarzan came first, that Bomba was hewn from the Ape Man's image? Let the Tarzan crowd prostrate themselves with creaking knees and aching joints in their own temples. Bomba was our Boy!

During adolescence Roy Rockwood had always been one of my favorite people. I pictured him seated at his desk, pen in hand, white shirt open at the throat, a bulldog pipe in his teeth. The creator of Bomba the Jungle Boy had a steady gaze, a firm mouth, a determined jaw. The walls of his study bristled with heads of leopard, grizzly and saber-tooth tiger. True, I had never actually seen a picture of the great author but I didn't have to. I just knew that's how he would look.

Discovery of the truth about Roy Rockwood left me a little stunned.

When you read a book you know it must have been written by somebody. You assume that the author is the somebody named on the cover. You take it for granted that this writer lives and breathes, that he eats breakfast every morning, argues occasionally with his wife, takes aspirin for his headaches, resents paying income tax and has a sour opinion of most politicians. In short, that he is a human being.

Now I learned from an unimpeachable source that Roy Rockwood wasn't a human being at all; he didn't exist, he never had existed. He was just as fictitious as Bomba the Jungle Boy. Like Nat Ridley, Jr., he was an imaginary author created by an author who didn't even write his own books. Roy Rockwood had less substance than a puff of smoke and by this time I wasn't feeling very sure about Edward Stratemeyer either.

I realized then that America is truly the land of opportunity. America, where every little boy knows he can grow up to be President if he isn't careful. Being Canadian, I couldn't qualify. But I could be Roy Rockwood, once my favorite author. In fact, I even had a choice. I could be Nat Ridley, Jr. if I felt like it. Where else in the world could that happen, but in America?

After work that night when the paper had gone to bed and the quiet of the cityroom was broken only by the occasional clatter of a teletype or an explosion of curses from the poker game down the hall, I settled down to study *Dave Fearless Among the Icebergs* (or *The Secret of the Eskimo Igloo*). The story opened on the Long Island estate of Amos Fearless, master diver, whose name was revered by all those brave men who went down into the sea in rubber suits and helmets. Mr. Fearless, "now old and feeble," had retired and turned over the family business to his son, Dave.

It had never dawned on me that deep-sea diving was big business, but apparently there was good money in it. Someone was always trying to recover valuable papers, jewelry or treasure of some kind from some sunken vessel. And navies in various parts of the world, it seemed, sometimes lost track of their submarines. Rather than suffer the embarrassment of a public search, they preferred to contract the job to a discreet and reliable firm such as A. Fearless & Son.

Dave Fearless, an introductory paragraph explained, was no novice in the diving business. Beginning as his father's surface assistant when he was a mere boy, he had been promoted to underwater helper and after serving his apprenticeship had become a fully qualified diver at the age of twenty-one. Somewhere at some time during his deep-sea career, Dave had acquired a friend, Bob Vilett, a young marine engineer. When the twosome weren't out diving for the firm, Bob was a house guest at the Long Island estate.

I recognized the ploy; Roy Rockwood was no fool. Any author who has a deep-sea diver for a hero runs into dialogue problems that are hard to believe. By the very nature of his solitary profession, a deep-sea diver will go around talking to himself most of the time. He may get used to it, but readers won't put up with these monologues for very long. They crave real live talk, and to make sure they got it Author Rockwood had to invent Sounding Board Vilett.

Chapter One, in fact, opened with the boys bouncing conversation off each other pretty briskly. They were discussing a letter Dave Fearless had received that day from a mariner named Captain Broadbeam, who explained that his boat, the *Swallow*, had been chartered by a group of scientists engaged on a research project in the Far North. He would like to have them aboard as members of his crew—one never knew when a diver might come in handy on an expedition of this kind.

As it happened, things had been a little dull in the diving business and the boys were free to go. Several months had gone by since anyone had come up with a map that pinpointed the location of a sunken treasure, and if any navy had lost track of a submarine the matter had been hushed up. After discussing Captain Broadbeam's invitation for the greater part of an evening, they agreed that it would be fun to go to the Arctic. They decided to get in touch with the skipper first thing in the morning. Then they turned in.

Author Rockwood didn't make a big thing of it, the Gay Nineties being long past, but he did mention casually that the chums occupied separate rooms. A nice touch, I thought.

The boys hadn't been asleep more than a few minutes before they were awakened by a man shouting for help. They leaped from their beds (separately) and discovered that the family garage was on fire. The cries for help continued.

"Someone," said Dave to Bob, "is trapped in that burning building."

"Who could it be?" said Bob to Dave.

End of Chapter One.

Hastening toward Chapter Two, I ran headlong into one of Edward Stratemeyer's more inspired inventions—the preceding volumes roundup. Chapter Two anticipated television by leading off with a commercial. Instead of urging the reader to go have a beer or a laxative, however, it plugged the other books:

> *While active preparations were under way to save the life of the stranger, our readers can be informed of other adventures of Dave Fearless and his chum Bob as recounted in earlier volumes of this series.*

One could see that Roy Rockwood was not the kind of man to lose his head in an emergency. The man burning to death in the garage could wait. With admirable composure Mr. Rockwood took time out to the extent of half a dozen pages to identify and synopsize the three books already published: *Dave Fearless After a Sunken Treasure* (or *The Rival Ocean Divers*), *Dave Fearless on a Floating Island* (or *The Cruise of the Treasure Ship*) and *Dave Fearless and the Cave of Mystery* (or *Adrift in the Pacific*).

In each book the lads engaged in perilous adventure, all the while pursued by a father-and-son pair of rascals named Lem and Bart Hankers. These were distant relatives who had inherited some hoary family feud that called for total ruination of Amos Fearless and his son. Each volume saw the Hankers vanquished, and each subsequent volume found them bouncing back with a brand-new repertoire of villainy. A persistent pair, they were obviously too dim-witted to get the message.

It took Author Rockwood about a thousand words to bring the history up to date. Although I realized that this digression was calculated to send the reader sprinting to the corner store to pick up any volumes he had missed, it had no such effect on me. I had a feeling that when you had read one Dave Fearless you had read them all. Besides, the Hankers — even in synopses — were beginning to be a little tiresome. When a villain is clobbered, I like him to stay clobbered.

Not until he concluded his sales pitch did Roy Rockwood get back to the burning garage. Fortunately the imprisoned stranger was still alive. Dave Fearless and Bob Vilett were able to rescue him, a little singed but none the worse for his ordeal.

I skimmed through the rest of the book, all twenty-three chapters.

The concluding chapter was a dandy. Dave and Bob were marooned on top of an iceberg. In the distance they could see the *Swallow* about to set sail for home and realized that Captain Broadbeam had given them up for lost. To add to their troubles, the polar bear showed up again. Dave shot the polar bear; but they weren't home free yet. They were still on top of the iceberg with no apparent way of getting down. Ingenuity prevailed. They skinned the polar bear. When the hide froze they used it as a sled and skimmed swiftly down the icy slope to sea level. Captain Broadbeam spied them through his telescope and soon they were all homeward bound.

A final paragraph assured readers that the adventures of Dave Fearless were not over by any means. They would be continued in the next volume of the series, which would be called *Dave Fearless Wrecked Among Savages* (or *The Captives of the Headhunters*).

I put down the book, deeply disappointed in Roy Rockwood. Even his most ardent admirer would have to admit that *Dave Fearless Among the Icebergs* was dreadful bilge. True, about fifteen years had passed since I read *Bomba, the Jungle Boy*, so I was prepared to admit that perhaps my tastes had changed with advancing age. On the other hand, here was evidence that Roy had slipped deplorably.

There was only one explanation: it couldn't be the same Roy Rockwood. And then I realized it probably *wasn't* the same Roy Rockwood. Mr. Stratemeyer's letter had made everything perfectly clear. Not everyone could write *Bomba, the Jungle Boy*, but almost anyone could be Roy Rockwood — including me.

Perhaps Nat Ridley, Jr. operated on a higher level; I opened *Tracked to the West* (or *Nat Ridley at the Magnet Mine*). Like the Dave Fearless book, it ran to twenty-five chapters and exactly 215 pages and like Dave Fearless, young Nat Ridley was supposed to be a youth of boundless courage. As it turned out, however, all his bravery was nothing more than downright lunacy; the boy detective was a boy lunkhead. He walked into ambushes that wouldn't have fooled a kid in kindergarten. He got shot at a lot and he was always getting captured by the scoundrels he sought to apprehend.

Despite all that, I did wind up with a certain amount of respect for Nat Ridley, Jr., whoever he was. Condemned to write a book about a namesake who was involved in a ramshackle plot that would have collapsed if anyone had used common sense anywhere in the first five chapters, he had completed the job with minimum physical or mental exertion.

He had managed this, I realized, by allowing very few words to a sentence and no more than one sentence to a paragraph. Each of his 215 pages had far more blank space than type. His dialogue was especially terse. A page of Nat Ridley, Jr. read like this:

> Nat Ridley ventured into the tunnel.
>
> He knew not what danger lurked in the darkness.
>
> "Anyone here?" he shouted.
>
> There was no answer.
>
> He gripped his pistol in one hand and his flashlight in the other as he moved forward.
>
> Suddenly he heard a familiar voice.
>
> "Drop your gun, Ridley."
>
> It was the voice of Adam Dangerfield.
>
> Nat Ridley quickly turned off the flashlight.
>
> Then he leaped to the other side of the tunnel.
>
> A shot rang out.
>
> Thanks to his quickness the bullet missed.
>
> He heard it hit the wall of the tunnel.
>
> "Dangerfield," he called out. "I advise you to surrender."
>
> "Why should I?"
>
> "Because the odds are against you. I have enough evidence to send you to the chair."
>
> A sneering laugh was the only reply.
>
> "Ha! You'll never catch me."
>
> Just then a strange roaring sound filled the tunnel.
>
> Then there was a brilliant light and the shriek of a locomotive whistle echoed in the narrow space.
>
> The Midnight Express had entered the tunnel!

I estimated that it probably took Nat Ridley, Jr. forty-five seconds to whip out that page of prose. Perhaps a whole minute if he typed with two fingers. On that basis he probably knocked out the whole book in less than four hours. Let's say a half day's work.

Viewed in that light, Edward Stratemeyer's proposition began to look attractive. To write a chapter of a book without having to worry about character, action or plot would call for little more than the ability to hit the keys of a typewriter. By staying on in the office for an hour or so after the day's work, I could probably hammer out a book in a week. Four books a month at $100 a book worked out to $400 a month, more than double my salary at the *Republican*.

Could I afford to turn it down?

It was true that neither of the sample books had even a smidgeon of merit. They had less content that a football bladder and no more style than a drunken camel. Garbage. But then, they didn't pretend to be works of literature. They were straightforward, cheap paperbacks for a public that would neither read nor relish anything better. And besides, I would be under no obligation to *read* the stuff. I would merely have to write it, hammer out the words in some reasonable progression so that they would make sense even if the plots didn't.

In fact it might even be fun. I talked myself into it and wrote to Edward Stratemeyer that night, telling him that I'd like to try my hand at a Dave Fearless book.

As the defendant said, I didn't know it was loaded.

CHAPTER 3:

Trial Run

Down the hall from the cityroom a cluttered little office was occupied by the newspaper's resident literary critic.

He was the first literary critic I had ever known and a big disappointment. He didn't rant and bellow. He didn't hurl books against the wall, roaring "bilge" and "rubbish." In fact, he insisted that he wasn't a literary critic at all. He was a reviewer. He merely read books and wrote about them. He was a gray little man, soft-spoken and so unobtrusive that no one ever saw him going into his office or leaving it. He just materialized there out of the dust and vanished the same way.

I can't even recall his name. A letter of inquiry to the current secretary of the *Republican* evoked a reply to the effect that no one at the *Republican* can recall his name either. Apparently after fifty years the quiet little fellow has vanished from the records. Maybe there is a lesson in this for book reviewers everywhere.

But he deserves a name, even if one must be invented for him. I shall call him Emerson C. Lowell, which has a fine New England ring to it. The C, of course, is for Cabot.

I looked in on him one afternoon. "Have you ever heard of a man called Edward Stratemeyer?" I asked.

Emerson C. Lowell gazed dreamily at the ceiling. "Sorry," he replied. "An author?"

"So I believe."

"It rings a bell somehow, but for the life of me I can't quite place the man." Another long look at the ceiling. "Something to do with Boy Scouts of America?"

"I wouldn't know."

"There might be something in the files. If it's important to you I'll have a look. But if I can't place him I think you can take it for granted that he hasn't published very much. Obscure, one might say."

Before I left, Mr. Lowell asked if I would care to review a couple of books for him and suggested that I take my choice from the volumes on his desk. I chose two. One was a contemporary novel and the other seemed to be a work of fiction by a clergyman. When I read it, I rejoiced. It was dreadful, so amateurish, so unbelievably bad that I had a fine time ridiculing the hell out of it in 500 very funny words. Mr. Lowell rejected my review.

"The point is," he said, "that it is much too easy to slate a book of that kind. And don't forget, it has probably been the poor fellow's lifetime ambition to get his book published. Granted that he has no talent, why hurt his feelings? Why ridicule him publicly? Just ignore the book."

He was that kind of reviewer.

"That author you inquired about," he said as he dropped my critique into the wastebasket. "Strathmore? Hasselmeyer?"

"Stratemeyer."

"Ah — that's why I couldn't locate it. I'll look again. I'm sure he had something to do with the Boys Scouts of America."

I was still unenlightened when I received a communication from Edward Stratemeyer a few days later. It consisted of an outline of two chapters of a book and a cryptic note suggesting that I try my hand at the two chapters by way of a trial run. He pointed out again that the assignment did not involve money, but added that if the two chapters met his standard, he would be pleased to offer me a contract to finish the book for a total payment of $100. All rights to the book would become the exclusive property of the Stratemeyer Syndicate.

The outline of this new, as yet unwritten volume, called *Dave Fearless Under the Ocean* (or *The Treasure of the Lost Submarine*) ran for three pages of single-spaced typescript and went something like this:

> *CHAP. 1 — Dave and Bob cruising off Long Island in launch Amos run into fog — mention first and second volumes of series — engine fails — ring reminds Bob of adventures on Volcano Island — mention other volumes — boys discuss Lem and Bart Hankers, believed dead — sound of foghorn is heard — ocean liner looms out of fog — collision seems inevitable.*
>
> *CHAP. 2 — Ship veers off in nick of time — boys hear warning bell and see lighthouse — fix engine — almost pile up on dangerous reef — night and darkness — searchlight suddenly reveals mass of wreckage dead ahead — launch crashes into wreckage and catches fire — boys dive into water — boat blows up — Dave looks for Bob.*

It went on for twenty-three more chapters, each loaded with action. When I put down the outline pages my head was swimming. My impression was that *Dave Fearless Under the Ocean* called for more perils and narrow escapes than a normal diver would encounter in several lifetimes. It all seemed pretty frantic.

I had sense enough to realize, however, that Mr. Stratemeyer was not hiring a critic. The creator of Dave Fearless knew what he wanted and was willing to pay for it. True, the payment would be modest even by the 1926 Consumers' Index, but it added up to more than two weeks' earnings at the *Republican*.

That night, after everyone had gone home for the day, a sheet of paper went into the typewriter and the keys began to clatter.

DAVE FEARLESS UNDER THE OCEAN

or

THE TREASURE OF THE LOST SUBMARINE

by

Roy Rockwood

CHAPTER 1
THE MENACE FROM THE MIST

After a few moments of meditation and perusal of the outline, the keys clattered again.

Dave Fearless looked out over the rolling waves and frowned as he saw a greasy cloud rolling in from the horizon.

"There's a fog coming up, Bob."

"Looks like it. Do you think we had better turn back?"

"Perhaps we should," agreed Dave. "We want to be back at Quanatack in time for supper."

The two chums, Dave Fearless, young deep-sea diver, and Bob Vilett, marine engineer, were cruising off the coast of Long Island in Dave's motor boat, the Amos. *Now, as Dave remarked, a fog was rising and they were a long way from home.*

So much for the narrative hook, in the standard tradition of pulp fiction. Get your story going on the first page with a passage of action and dialogue. Introduce your chief character in a dramatic situation.

But this wasn't pulp fiction. This was a book series. The outline stipulated mention of the first and second volumes. It was time to leave Dave and Bob in the fog for a while and give a summary of *Dave Fearless After a Sunken Treasure*, thoughtfully provided by Mr. Stratemeyer. Not too much. Just enough to let the young readers know where they stood, and enough to tempt them into blowing their dimes on the whole series. Then, back to the fog.

"We can't depend on the weather at this time of year," said Dave Fearless.

Apparently they couldn't depend on the *Amos* either, because . . .

Hardly had he spoken when the steady throbbing of the engine became slower. It coughed jerkily for a moment and died.

"I thought something would happen," said Bob.

After all, the kid had been out with Dave Fearless before.

Dave Fearless prepared to overhaul the engine.
"The engine is dead and a fog is coming up."
"Also the waves are getting rougher and it will be night
before we know it," said Bob.
"Hold my ring for a while, will you?" asked Dave as he
delved into the engine.

Just why Dave is fooling around with the engine when he has a qualified marine engineer on board may bother a few sharp youngsters, but he is the hero, it's his boat and anyhow that's what it says in the outline. And as for quibblers who may feel that the weather recap is redundant, remember that readers have been distracted by the summaries of Volume One and Two for the past five pages.

The reference to the ring is pretty neat because it happens to be a memento of another past adventure, the great Volcano Island affair and the search for the blue diamonds, one of which has adorned Dave's finger ever since. Clearly it calls for a reference to Volume Seven, *Dave Fearless on Volcano Island*, which naturally leads to a recap of Volume Eight, *Dave Fearless Captured by Apes*. And, having gone this far, we may as well go on to suggest the thrills and excitement to be found in Volume Nine, *Dave Fearless and the Mutineers*, which brings us right up to date because Volume Nine immediately precedes the volume in hand.

Into the fog again.

"I don't know where Bart Hankers can be," observed
Dave, "but Lem Hankers is dead. You remember he fell
overboard when he tried to throw me over the rail."

Apparently the faithful readers aren't the only ones who need to have memories jogged once in a while. Even Bob must be a little on the dim-witted side if he has to be reminded of this incident. But he picks up his cue with commendable promptitude.

"Bart won't bother us any more," said Bob. "Now that
his father is gone, I don't think we need bother about him."

Little does he know! Edward Stratemeyer is not one to

drown a perfectly good villain in Volume Nine of an established series.

"No," said Dave, "but I think we'd better worry about this fog."

All is clear sailing from here on to the end of the chapter. Clear sailing for Roy Rockwood, that is, but not for Dave Fearless and chum. The fog gets worse. Dave is still fooling around with the engine and Bob is doubtless restraining a natural impulse to show him what he is doing wrong. Roy Rockwood restrains his impulse to write:

"Oh, come on, you idiot! You'll flood the bloody engine. Move over. Let somebody who knows what he's doing have a whack at it."

Instead, he writes:

Suddenly they heard the booming of a foghorn, alarmingly close at hand.

"A ship!" cried Dave.

"Ahoy there!" shouted Bob.

A great dark shape loomed out of the fog.

"We're done for!" gasped Dave.

Like a mountain, the ship bore down on them through the dense mist. They were right in its path.

End of Chapter One. It was three o'clock in the morning.

The next night I dug out Mr. Stratemeyer's outline from a desk drawer, refreshed my memory of the events scheduled to take place in Chapter Two, and got back to work.

Dave Fearless and chum were not run down by the ship after all. At the last moment—"in the nick of time" I wrote—the vessel veered off into the night. Naturally, the boys "breathed sighs of relief." But they weren't out of trouble yet—that pesky engine wouldn't turn over. There is nothing like a stiff onshore gale, a pitch-black night, and the sound of surf on rocks to goose even an amateur mechanic into superhuman efforts. Dave got the engine started! Since I didn't have even the vaguest knowledge of marine engines myself, it seemed wise to avoid details. No point in making Roy Rockwood sound like a fool. He just *did* it.

And then, faithful to the outline, the lads came close to piling up on a dangerous reef, their searchlight revealed a mass of wreckage dead ahead, the launch crashed into the wreckage and caught fire, the boys dove into the water and the boat blew up. At the end of the chapter Dave was swimming around, looking vainly for his chum.

That ended the trial run. I mailed the two chapters to Stratemeyer and awaited his verdict with confidence. I felt that the chapters were every bit as good as anything in *Dave Fearless Among the Icebergs*. Better, in fact. I pictured Edward Stratemeyer tossing his hat in the air and shouting, "Hurray! I have found my man!"

Shortly after, the quietly zealous Emerson C. Lowell invited me into his office to reveal some information he had uncovered on our mysterious Mr. Stratemeyer.

"Have you ever heard of *The Rover Boys*?" he asked.

"Of course. I read a couple of them when I was a kid . . . Stratemeyer wrote *The Rover Boys*?"

"Among other things. I haven't read any of them, of course. I understand that some twenty titles in the series have sold upward of five million copies."

"But they're awful!"

"Naturally. You see, Stratemeyer took over from Alger."

"Horatio Alger?"

"There is only one Alger."

"What do you mean by saying Stratemeyer took over?"

"There seems to be a little controversy about this matter, that is, if one can say the issue is worth being controversial about. Before Alger died in 1900 it seems he had published more than 100 books, which sold in the millions. Biggest selling writer in America, no question about it. But after he died, more Alger books came out. There seemed to be no stopping them. About eleven new Alger books appeared before it was revealed that Stratemeyer had a hand in them. Stratemeyer used to be one of Alger's editors, besides being a writer of the same kind of stuff himself, and a friend of Alger. He said Alger had appointed him his literary executor and that the new books were written from outlines found in Alger's papers."

Mr. Stratemeyer, however, had another claim to eminence.

"It seems," said Lowell, "that Stratemeyer runs a fiction factory."

"A factory?"

Lowell explained that Edward Stratemeyer was responsible — "or to blame, if you like" — for most of the inexpensive juvenile books published in America.

"He sets up ideas for series, sells the ideas to publishers and then hires people to write the books. Nearly all the popular juvenile series such as Tom Swift and the like come straight from Stratemeyer's assembly line. Mass-produced. Mass-merchandized. Typical American idea."

"That's very interesting," I said, but didn't bother to explain my interest.

Mr. Lowell rummaged through a desk drawer and handed me a pamphlet entitled "The Winnetka Survey."

"The head of the Winnetka public school system — that's in Illinois — made a survey in 1914 for the American Library Association. Nearly 40,000 pupils in thirty-four cities were asked about their reading preferences. The results were alarming. The kids voted almost unanimously for junk." He checked the pamphlet. "Ninety-eight percent."

"*The Rover Boys* were right up there?"

"Not quite. *Tom Swift* nosed them out."

"Tom Swift, the boy inventor. Victor Appleton, author."

Mr. Lowell nodded his head in agreement "I have it on good authority that Victor Appleton is Edward Stratemeyer. These books are published in series. They sell for fifty cents. All the series books swept the Winnetka Survey. Apparently that's what young America is reading nowadays," he sighed.

"Better than nothing."

"I doubt it. The argument is that they encourage the reading habit and that when youngsters outgrow *The Rover Boys* and *Tom Swift* they'll go on to bigger and better things."

"It sounds reasonable."

"I'm afraid they merely go on to Harold Bell Wright, who wrote *The Winning of Barbara Worth*, which qualifies him to be regarded as our very worst writer. Frankly," he confided, "the more I learn about the publishing business the more I wonder what I'm doing in this office."

"Maybe the Winnetka Survey will do some good."

"Some libraries have banned the fifty-cent juveniles. You realize what that means."

"The kids will read better books."

"The kids will stop going to libraries, where they might be exposed to better books. Instead of taking out a *Tom Swift* on loan they'll buy it. The sales will boom. I wish you hadn't brought up the subject." Mr. Lowell reached for his hat. "I find the whole situation so revolting that it will take a couple of stiff drinks to restore my faith in the future of the Republic. Will you join me in a little trip around the corner?"

In the speakeasy Mr. Lowell insisted on proposing a toast to the damnation of Edward Stratemeyer. To refuse would have involved explanations I didn't care to give at the moment. In my turn I proposed a toast to F. Scott Fitzgerald, who had recently published *The Great Gatsby*, and Mr. Lowell cheered up immediately and decided that American literature was flourishing in spite of everything.

CHAPTER 4:

Goodbye Springfield

In the next week, while awaiting the verdict on the first chapters of *Dave Fearless Under the Ocean* (which seemed uncommonly delayed in view of its obvious merits), I came close to being involved in one of the great news stories of the century.

"Have you ever covered an execution?" asked Walsh.

"Once," I told him.

This was when I worked in northern Ontario, for the *Sudbury Star*. It involved a homeless wanderer who had been kicked off a train in midwinter and found refuge in a trapper's cabin. The trapper was old, lonely and glad of company. Liquor was forbidden by law in that area and the trapper, lacking a bottle of rye with which to cement friendship, fished out a bottle of hair tonic, a potation which can blow the mind. When the refugee woke up the next morning, he found his host lying dead beside a stick of firewood.

Shocked and contrite, unable to remember anything that had happened, he sought out the police and gave himself up. At the trial, much to the distress of his court-appointed counsel, he insisted on pleading guilty. It was his bad luck to be born fifty years too soon, because they hanged him.

"I saw him in his cell half an hour before the drop," I told Walsh. "I saw him on the undertaker's slab half an hour later. I've been against capital punishment ever since. That's all it takes."

"But the M.E. says you're to cover Chapman in Hartford tonight."

"Thanks for the honor but I'd rather not."

"Sorry. Anyhow, you'll find this one different. Historic, in any case."

The historic interest lay in the fact that the machine-age had produced a brand-new invention which was to be unveiled in Hartford Prison. It was a hanging machine. Its first occupant was to be Gerald Chapman, notorious bank thief and mail robber, who had gunned down a guard while trying to get away with a million dollars.

The principle of the invention lay in reverse action. Instead of stepping on a trapdoor and being dropped to his doom, Chapman was to sit in a chair and then be snapped aloft by the rope. Penologists were greatly interested in the new method, which promised to revolutionize the art of painless execution. Kind-hearted citizens protested that it was barbarous. The old-fashioned way, they said, was much preferable.

Walsh gave me a ticket for this event. Although the execution was to be in Connecticut, and Springfield was in Massachusetts, the *Republican* was entitled to one of the few reserved seats.

I didn't look forward to the assignment and I spent the rest of the afternoon worrying lest I should faint and disgrace myself.

Jacobsen, the police reporter, came over and congratulated me. "Lucky you," he said. "Do you realize tickets are so scarce the New York papers are screaming mad? They're offering as high as two thousand bucks to anyone who'll give up his ticket."

Just then Walsh called me over. "It's off," he said.

"Chapman got a reprieve?"

"Oh, no. But upstairs there's been a change of heart. The decision is that the *Republican* won't cover it."

"I'll try to swallow my disappointment," I told him and went back to my desk. "Now then," I said briskly to Jacobsen, "how do I go about selling this valuable ticket? Shall I call the *Graphic*?"

Emil Gavreau's *Graphic* specialized in Great Pix, often phony, like the Earl Carroll scandal when a chorus girl stripped and got into a bathtub full of champagne, or the wedding night of Daddy Browning, the old millionaire who married a fifteen-year-old called Peaches.

"The *Graphic*, by all means," said Jacobsen. "In fact I wouldn't let them off the hook for two thousand. Start the bidding at five."

Walsh appeared again. "Oh, by the way," he said. "I forgot about the ticket. Let's have it."

"Who gets it?" I inquired dismally.

"Nobody gets it. My orders are to send it back with our regrets."

I gave him the ticket.

"Tough," said Jacobsen. "Let's go around the corner for a beer."

"Just one," I said. "I had planned to invite everybody in the office but I haven't got more than forty cents."

The next morning, reluctantly sober and well rested, I read the out-of-town newspapers on the exchange desk with more than usual interest. The new hanging machine — to say nothing of the unfortunate Chapman — had gone off in fine style. The story got front-page coverage everywere and the *Graphic* excelled itself with imaginatively synthetic pix.

I wasn't sorry I had missed the historic event. It is one thing to read about such an affair but to stand and watch a human being yanked into eternity is another matter entirely. Two of the reporters had passed out. Some observers said they didn't think the hanging machine was such a vast improvement after all. Scientific progress is all very well but perhaps it should be devoted to better ends.

Of more importance to me was a long envelope in the mail rack. It contained The Verdict.

Stratemeyer's reply was restrained in tone. If he admired the opening chapters of *Dave Fearless Under the Ocean* and thought the material was great stuff, he conquered any impulse to say so. Instead, he merely wrote that the chapters were "satisfactory" and instructed me to go ahead and finish the book. This was just as well. I was so confident of the outcome that I had gone blithely ahead with the outline anyhow and had made a net gain of five more chapters by the time his letter arrived.

Once I got the hang of it, chapters of this kind came easily —so easily, in fact, that it seemed in order to bang out another and another without stopping for breath. Mr. Stratemeyer's go-ahead inspired me with such enthusiasm that I was encouraged to step up the pace to two chapters a session, working often until four in the morning. This went on for about a week.

I was getting by on so little sleep that Mr. Arbuthnot, my landlord, began to worry. He cornered me at the foot of the stairs one noontime when I emerged, glassy eyed, to face the day. Mr. Arbuthnot had decided it was time he voiced his concern. He had always prided himself, he said, on being a man who minded his own business. Nevertheless, he took a friendly interest in his lodgers; as a good Christian he would be failing in his duty if he lacked concern for the well-being of the young men who dwelt under his roof. Consequently, it grieved him to realize he was harboring one who was clearly on the road to perdition.

"Drink," said Mr. Arbuthnot, wagging an admonishing finger, "has been the undoing of many a promising lad away from home for the first time."

I tried to tell him that I had been away from home for about five years, but he waved this aside as immaterial.

"Drink," he persisted, "destroys the health. It rots the liver, softens the brain. It's bad for one's reputation. And besides, it's expensive."

I protested mildly that he was mistaken. I didn't drink. Privately, I considered that the occasional pint of prohibition beer in the speakeasy around the corner from the *Republican* office didn't really count.

"Now, now," said Mr. Arbuthnot reprovingly. "Don't make things worse by denying it. Night after night I hear you stumbling in here at the most dreadful hours. Half past four— even five — in the morning. Disturbing everyone."

It was true, I conceded, that occasionally I barked my shins on the steps while groping roomward and that I had created a commotion by falling upstairs in the early hours that very morning. But I denied the imputation that these mishaps were attributable to strong drink.

"I work late," I protested.

Mr. Arbuthnot clucked incredulously. "Nobody works *that* late. Have you looked in the mirror lately?"

"This morning when I shaved."

"Bloodshot eyes. Pale. Haggard. You're heading for a collapse, my boy. Burning the candle. And, of course, apart from the ruinous effects of alcohol there is another evil I needn't mention." Mr. Arbuthnot's eyes gleamed. He jabbed my chest with a phallic forefinger. "Loose women!" he said in a hushed voice.

"But I don't know any loose women. I wouldn't have time for them anyway."

"Now, now! We're all human, my boy. But that kind of female company can do you no good. Understand what I mean?"

I understood very well. By common report the Twenties had become a Decade of Decadence. Girls rolled their stockings and revealed their knees. Clergymen brayed their alarm over a complete breakdown of morals among the young. Newspapers and magazines ran interesting pieces to the effect that the postwar generation was getting drunk and fornicating all over the place.

Probably I hadn't been looking in the right places, but so far I had found little evidence of these deplorable conditions in Springfield, Massachusetts.

"You're wrong, Mr. Arbuthnot," I said.

He sniffed skeptically. "You owe it to the young woman you'll marry some day to change your ways before it's too late. If she could see you now! The red-rimmed eyes. The signs of dissipation."

He shuffled away, shaking his head and clucking. I felt put upon, and took a look in the hall mirror before going out.

Maybe I did look a little jaded, but the old gentleman's assumptions were highly unjust. Who wouldn't look a bit frayed around the edges on less than six hours' sleep a night?

Under my expanded work schedule, which meant that I didn't emerge into the light of day before twelve o'clock noon, I regularly ate breakfast at a service club. The Optimists, Kiwanians, Lions and Rotarians apparently relished the Kimball fare and did not complain about its lack of variety, but there is something about a chicken croquette that just naturally gets a day off to a poor start.

So few "stars" passed through town that I was glad later in the week to spend a couple of hours interviewing De Wolf Hopper, a gigantic musical comedy star with a red toupee and an improbable complexion. His craggy face looked as if it had been copperplated. In a manner of speaking, this was true. Mr. Hopper confided to me that some fool doctor had once ministered to him for a minor ailment and erred by putting a copper solution in the injection treatments. "I was lucky to escape with my life," he said.

Mr. Hopper was not a difficult man to interview. He reminisced nonstop for three hours and appeared to enjoy himself thoroughly. I was so fascinated by his enormous nose, which looked as if it had gone through the penny bath at the United States Mint, that when I checked my notes in the *Republican* cityroom that evening I found them lacking in continuity. However, I wrote the interview—about a column and a half—and was deflated when Bill Walsh, scowling, cut it to 500 words.

That night Walsh lingered after closing time, apparently absorbed in the bulldog edition. I fooled around and did a little housecleaning.

"Why didn't you tell me you were going to interview that windbag?" Walsh asked abruptly. "I'd have steered you off."

"I'm sorry you didn't like it."

"I liked it the first time. But that was about eight years ago. Every time Hopper shows up in town he corners some innocent and talks his ear off. It's always the same interview."

"I liked him. He gave me a ticket to his show, *The Student Prince*, for my night off. What's more, he promised to recite 'Casey at the Bat' during intermission as a personal favor just for me."

Walsh sighed. "Just for you," he said, shaking his head. "Why the performance wouldn't be legal if Hopper didn't recite 'Casey at the Bat.' He *always* recites 'Casey at the Bat.' He has been reciting 'Casey at the Bat' since 1888. Men with clubs wouldn't stop him. It's probably written into his contract. If De Wolf came to town starring in *Hamlet* he would recite 'Casey at the Bat' as a little specialty following his scene with the First Gravedigger."

I was beginning to think that Walsh was a little prejudiced against De Wolf Hopper. "Don't mind me, anyway," he said, looking over the top of his paper. "Why don't you go ahead with your novel?"

"Novel?"

"One of the janitors told me. You're writing a book, aren't you?"

I wouldn't have pleaded guilty to a novel but I admitted I was writing a book.

"How much have you done?"

"Fourteen chapters. It's almost finished."

"Fourteen *chapters*?"

"I write fast."

"You mean you write quickly," said Walsh, ever the good deskman. He got up and reached for his hat. "Well I'll be damned." He went over to the rack for his jacket and looked back. "Know something? I'll bet I've seen a hundred reporters come and go since I came to work here. At least ninety-five of them have tried to write a book. And not a damned one of them ever got past the third chapter."

"I'm afraid this one isn't exactly a work of art."

"So what ? But fourteen chapters! Even if you never get it finished you've broken a *Republican* record. And if you do get it finished and published I want an autographed copy. Promise?"

"Yes, sir."

"Fourteen chapters? Wow!"

Bill Walsh left for the night. Cheered, I thrust a sheet of paper into the typewriter. City editors aren't easily awed.

The boys were about to resume their search for the lost submarine. This was scheduled to involve an encounter with a school of man-eating sharks, so I hammered out Chapter Fifteen — The Man-eaters and went to work.

> The Falcon was at anchor.
>
> Dave Fearless and Bob prepared to cast off the small boat they planned to use in their search.
>
> "I'll be in such suspense until I see you again," Mrs. Harlow called out to them.
>
> "Good luck," cried Lola and Pearl as the boat set out.
>
> "We'll be back in time for lunch," promised Bob.

Like hell they would.

According to outline, Dave was scheduled to locate the submarine all right, but first he was to get himself entangled in a mass of deadly seaweed. Duly rescued by Bob, he would then engage in battle with the man-eating sharks to justify the chapter title.

The boys wouldn't get back to the Falcon for at least three chapters. They would miss their lunch. But so, of course, would the sharks.

> "I'm nervous every minute Dave is away," declared Lola. "He runs such dangers walking around on the bottom of the ocean. He might meet another octopus."

Lola needn't have worried. We've already used that octopus character in Chapter Eleven. In the Dave Fearless series I am rationed to one octopus per book. If Dave does meet one, it will turn out to be a peace-loving octopus. He will merely wave to Dave in friendly fashion — using all eight arms — and go on about his business.

But the lethal seaweed is waiting.

And so are the man-eating sharks.

As Lola says, you can run into a lot of dangers walking around on the bottom of the ocean.

Clackety-clack-clack-clackety-clack.

At three a.m. by the office clock, Bob hauled Dave out of the seaweed and the chapter ended as the boys met up with the school of sharks. I steamed right into Chapter Sixteen, the boys routed the sharks in less than 1,200 words, and I let myself into Mr. Arbuthnot's respectable lodging house a few minutes after four.

Three nights later Dave Fearless and his chum found the submarine. How? They just kept walking the ocean floor until they bumped into it. As simple as that. The lesson for young readers was that given patience and a little luck, to say nothing of the ability to fend off seaweed, sharks, octopi and Hankers, a couple of diligent lads can accomplish practically anything. They retrieved a mysterious red box containing a million dollars' worth of diamonds from the submarine. This made Mrs. Harlow very happy. She had never come out and actually said so, but no one could have blamed her if she harbored suspicions that her husband had pawned the diamonds and decamped with the proceeds.

Only one question remained: where, in fact, *was* the missing Mr. Harlow? This was answered in timely fashion on the next-to-last page of the final chapter. A wireless message reached the *Falcon*. It was from Mr. Harlow, of all people, and it came from the Harlow estate on Long Island, of all places. Mr. Harlow was safe and sound. He had not, in fact, been on board the submarine at all when it went down. His subsequent delay in getting in touch was easily explained; he had been marooned on a desert island. Like a good wife, Mrs. Harlow accepted this. I was strongly tempted to write that she had a pretty thoughtful look on her face when she read the remarkable dispatch but it would have been painting the lily. It stood to reason that good old-man Harlow was in for a pretty exhaustive cross-examination when she got home. Desert island, indeed!

Once again, the rascally Hankers had been foiled. The

Falcon got under way again, while Dave, Bob, Lola and Pearl enjoyed deck sports of an antiseptic nature under the indulgent eye of Mrs. Harlow.

A final page went into the typewriter.

> *"Well, you located the lost submarine," said Bob to Dave. "Now all our troubles are at an end."*
>
> *But Bob was mistaken.*
>
> *More adventures were in store for him and the young diver, and what some of them were will be related in the next volume of this series, to be called:* Dave Fearless in the Black Jungle (*or* Lost Among the Cannibals), *a weird tale of savage life in the unknown portions of the Amazonian forests.*

I heaved a gusty sigh as the typewriter clattered "The End" and I pulled the final page from the typewriter. The manuscript, unread, unrevised and uncorrected, went into a large, brown envelope which, in turn, went into the outgoing mail basket. There wasn't even a carbon copy. The postal service would have been flattered by this manifestation of utter faith; any professional writer would have been horrified.

My first book!

"A poor thing, but not entirely my own," I thought ruefully; one had to admit the Stratemeyer contribution.

When Mr. Stratemeyer handed down his verdict he allowed, with his customary restraint, that *Dave Fearless Under the Ocean* was "a lively narrative." He didn't say he was unable to put down the manuscript until he finished it but, after all, he was in a position to know how it came out anyway. More to the point, he sent along a check for $100.

I somehow expected that a check from a big syndicate would be an impressively gaudy affair, in several colors perhaps, with the amount typed in capital letters and at least a couple of splashy signatures including that of a Comptroller. Mr. Stratemeyer's check, however, was as modest in size as it was in value and he had written it personally from date to signature in crabbed handwriting that resembled that of my grandfather. Obviously an old-fashioned man who didn't bother trying to impress people.

Even more to the point, he sent along another three-page outline of the next book in the saga. This was to be called *Dave Fearless in the Black Jungle* (or *Lost Among the Cannibals*). He wanted to know if I would take on an assignment every month and make myself available for work on other series.

That did it.

By working full time for the Stratemeyer Syndicate I could easily whack out four books a month, double my income and get some sleep at night. There would even be time to spare for higher endeavors, literature in the Joseph Conrad vein, for example.

Clearly I couldn't afford to go on working for the *Republican*.

Bill Walsh accepted a week's notice with no visible grief. He remarked that a promotion to feature writing had been in the wind but that he never tried to hold a man who wanted to leave.

"Where to now? New York?"

"Back to Canada."

"Why Canada, for God's sake?"

It was difficult to explain. I liked what little I had seen of the United States. I liked Americans — outgoing, gregarious, generous. They never thought there was something discreditable about being young. In Canada the prevailing attitude assumed that no man under forty had an ounce of brains or an opinion worth a damn.

My countrymen, on the whole, were a dour lot, full of deprecation and mistrust, overly cautious, resistant to change and much given to religion, which meant that most of them were glum and disposed to frown on any kind of pleasure. Only the European immigrants and French-Canadians seemed to know how to enjoy themselves.

The climate, marvelous at its best, was miserable at its worst. There were many weeks when the country lay bleakly under a blanket of cloud, which probably accounted for the habitual sternness of the inhabitants. People spent a good deal of their money merely trying to keep warm.

And culture was primitive. It seemed that all our poets were professors, that all our novelists were clergymen or pious housewives, and that all our artists — especially a peculiar bunch known as the Group of Seven—were downright crazy. A Canadian book or a Canadian painting was automatically worthless until pronounced otherwise by some foreigner.

This was Canada in the Twenties.

Clearly, the decision didn't add up. But how does one explain the subtle, magnetic attraction of one's native land, the longing for the familiar, for the wilderness cabin that I had lived in the previous summer, the rocks and sandy beach of the bay, the sparkling waters and green shores of the lake in the strong northern sunshine?

That night I unfolded the outline of *Dave Fearless in the Black Jungle*. No point in reading the whole thing. It would only confuse me and might bring on an attack of the jim-jams. A chapter at a time was about all one could take.

The outline called for twenty-three chapters, each representing about six pages of typescript. By putting on a little extra pressure, such as hammering out half a dozen chapters on my day off, the book could be finished the day before I left the *Republican*. Nice timing.

Deep-sea divers who go adventuring in the jungles of the Amazon may as well leave their gear at home. All those ropes and helmets merely clutter up the trip. As I ploughed my way through the outline night after night, I found that the boys had no opportunity to exercise their special underwater talents. They were much too busy fighting off the boa constrictors and cannibals that, as everyone knows, infest the Brazilian boondocks in such numbers that they have practically become public nuisances.

When these encounters became a little repetitious, Roy Rockwood, all on his own, decided to liven things up by abandoning the outline briefly to devise a couple of chapters of his own about a man-eating tropical tree. The botanical curiosity was introduced in Chapter Fourteen when Dave and Bob, motivated by sheer Christian charity, tried to rescue villainous Captain Riley from a tribe of savages. As occasionally happens when good Christians get carried away by noble intentions, their effort backfired. The savages grabbed Dave and Bob too, and set the trio up for immediate execution.

The situation looked pretty bad until rescue came from an unexpected quarter! Captain Riley went insane with fear, and the savages were so puzzled by Riley's irrational antics that they concluded that he was possessed by evil spirits. They forthwith postponed the executions on religious grounds and decided that Riley needed the services of a medicine man.

Writers of pulp fiction soon learn that nothing should ever happen easily.

A medicine man? These savages were backward: they didn't have a medicine man in residence. The nearest practitioner lived in another village and did not, of course, make house calls. And thus, the stage was set for several pages of perilous jungle journey.

But what perils? When you have used up your quota of boa constrictors, panthers and quicksands, you have to think hard. It's a bit of a challenge, but any resourceful writer can rise to it.

A tree that eats people alive!

I felt that I had arrived as a professional when I came up with that one.

It was Bob who was collared by a branch of this tree — hitherto unknown to arboriculturalists—when he accidentally brushed against it.

> *The more he struggled, the more he was imprisoned, for every time he touched a fresh twig or branch in his convulsive efforts to liberate himself, it coiled swiftly about any part of his body with which it came in contact.*

The savages, of course, were utterly useless in this emergency. They stood around like a pack of lunkheads, gibbering with fear as they pointed to the skeletons of previous victims in the upper branches.

At this point Dave Fearless lived up to this name. He went after the tree with a spear. Naturally, he too became entrapped when the tree apparently regarded him as a tasty morsel for dessert. It was nip and tuck before he found a vital spot and stabbed the tree to death just as both lads were turning blue.

Compared to the man-eating tree — an innovation which has always made me proud — the remaining chapters of the book were dull. *Dave Fearless in the Black Jungle* creaked and bumped its way to some kind of conclusion, with everyone back on the yacht and the villains foiled again.

The script was packed off to Mr. Stratemeyer on my last day at the *Republican*. The final pay envelope financed a farewell session at the neighborhood speakeasy, attended by colleagues who felt that any newspaperman who had actually finished a book — even a Dave Fearless — was somehow deserving of recognition.

Even Emerson C. Lowell showed up and got mildly jingled on beer. He pressed my hand, wished me well, and asked for my address which he entered in a small notebook. I would be hearing from him, he promised, because he had uncovered a good deal of information about my Mr. Hasselmeyer, which he would send by mail. "And I was right all along," said Mr. Lowell, proudly. "About the Boy Scouts, I mean."

The great thing about a speakeasy was that it was not obliged to observe a closing hour set by law and because it was a Saturday night the festivities went on into the Sabbath. The Great Roy Rockwood Farewell wound up in a tumultous invasion of Mr. Arbuthnot's lodging house at dawn when three companions, loyal to the end, decided to help pack my trunk. This operation, conducted to a rousing version of *Auld Lang Syne*, threw the whole place into an uproar.

I have blurred recollections of Mr. Arbuthnot in his nightshirt, bellowing with wrath; of alarms and excursions as fellow lodgers came groping out of their cells to inquire what on earth was going on; of scuffling that erupted when the City Hall man had to be restrained from throwing Mr. Arbuthnot out the window; of the cop who arrived, recognized us as fellow speakeasy pals of a few hours earlier and instantly departed in search of reinforcements, never to be seen again; of the glorious finale when the Churches and Obits man missed the top step while lugging out the trunk and we all went bumbling and crashing down the stairs, trunk included, while Mr. Arbuthnot howled denunciations from the landing and quoted from the Book of Job.

By six a.m. I was on my way back to Canada.

CHAPTER 5:

A Book Is a Book Is a Buck

In my cabin on Lake Ramsey in the nickel mining country 300 miles north of Toronto, I was a free man again.

No alarm clock to shatter slumber in the morning. Instead, a drowsy wakening to bird calls in the woods, the cry of a loon on the lake, the gentle drumming of rain on the roof.

No need to hurry any more. Three miles away, the *Sudbury Star* office is opening for the day. I worked there for five years but its concerns are no longer mine. This cabin, with its clean air and clean water and green woods, is home. I love the place because it represents total freedom.

I had lived there the previous summer when I burned all my bridges and struck out on a freelance career, sharing the cabin with my friend Mel Beath, world war veteran still in his twenties. Both broke, we lived on beer and beans supplemented by occasional handouts from the sympathetic mothers of our girl friends, and thought it one of the finest summers of our lives. Now Beath is in a Muskoka hospital, doomed by tuberculosis, and I miss him.

From the screened veranda I inspect the day. Mist rising lazily from the water, the offshore island shedding its shroud. A fish jumps and the rings widen. A duck and her small brood sail sedately close to shore in the curve of the bay where the water reflects the overhang of birches. The beach lies yellow in sunshine.

Cedar kindling crackles in the stove. Coffee and water are in the pot. I run down to the beach, the sand warm and smooth underfoot, the shock of cold water. Back to the cabin for a rubdown and I dress for the day — pants and a pair of moccasins. Shave? The hell with it.

Outside again to the patch of low bushes among the rocks — drops of dew on the leaves, fat clusters of blueberries in the shade — and in a few minutes I have enough for breakfast. At the back of the cabin I visit my cooler, a bushel basket embedded in the earth on the shady side, with chunks of ice protected by a burlap bag, shielding milk, butter and bacon, cool and fresh.

A nervous chipmunk watches inquisitively from atop the woodpile. Down the dappled trail waddles Geraldine, my pet, followed by her three little ones, nose to tail in solemn single file, enchanting in the manner of all small creatures. Of course, this may not be my Geraldine of the previous summer, but one of her progeny. It is not easy to identify a skunk. She is beautiful, her sleek, black fur accentuated by the clean, white stripe on her back. We have reached an understanding. If I behave myself and allow her to rummage unmolested among the tin cans in the trash box, she will behave herself too. But no sudden moves, remember! If her youngsters become frightened, Geraldine is capable of drastic action. She ignores me, and goes about her business with dignity.

Back in the kitchen I put strips of bacon in the frying pan, drench the blueberries with milk, douse them with brown sugar. Soon the eggs are spluttering, the bacon is crisp, the toast is brown, the coffee is ready. Out on the veranda I eat while watching the melting mist. It isn't always so warm, so bright and peaceful, but even on stormy days when the wind roars in the trees and big waves crash on the beach and the distant shore is lost in rain, there is contentment here.

I finish my breakfast, lug my typewriter out to the veranda and light the first pipe of the day. It is time to face facts.

There is an outline at hand: *Dave Fearless Near the South Pole*, (or *The Giant Whales of Snow Island*). Stratemeyer will send another as soon as the script is finished. Maybe two or three books a month. Even at 1926 living costs I can make a living turning out material full-time for Stratemeyer. But what about the magazine stories which could lead to better things?

Setting down the words of a Dave Fearless book cannot be called writing. Granted that some technical facility is required to translate an outline into twenty-three chapters, there is no getting away from the truth. This isn't writing; it is merely typing. Hack work at best. There is no solace in the thought that thousands of my contemporaries, from popular romancers to ghosts who write speeches for politicians, are in the same league. Hack is hack.

At the same time there has to be some money to pay for beans, beer, food, coffee and tobacco. The cabin costs only $100 a year. Another $100 a month will cover the rest. That equals one book a month for Stratemeyer. No more. An hour a day for Dave Fearless. The rest of the time will be spent on Better Stuff.

I slip a sheet of paper in the machine, type "Chapter One — Attacked from Ambush," and whip into the opening dialogue:

> "Dave, you may think I'm crazy but I'm sure I saw the Hankers last night hanging around this dock."
> There was no mistaking the earnestness in the tone of Bob Vilett as he spoke to his chum, Dave Fearless. The two stood on the deck of the motor yacht. . . .

It was only nine o'clock that morning when I wrote, "At the same instant, something struck Dave Fearless on the back of the head. Then everything went black."

That did it for Chapter One. I put the typed sheets in a folder and turned to a story I had in mind, based on the life of an old prospector I had known in this region, a man who had discovered half a dozen big mines and profited from none of them, a man who "knew rock" as he said. It was just the sort of thing *Adventure* would snap up, I felt sure, as I broke the plot of "Hill of Gold" down into chapters.

There would be no whales in this yarn. Such animal life as

the old prospector encountered would present no threat to his life. The weather would be clement, conspicuous by absence of typhoons, droughts or hurricanes. Light local showers, maybe, but nothing worse. If any old enemies showed up he would avoid them. If he came upon a glacial crevasse he would stay the hell away from it and keep out of trouble. If, by some unlikely chance, he sighted a herd of giant whales he would leave them alone and wait until they went away, the sensible way to deal with whales.

Later that afternoon, the story drafted and headway made on the opening chapter, I sat back, cheered, feeling that I was back in my rightful business.

Never again would I work for a master, by hour, by day, by week or by year. Perhaps I had neither the talent nor the ability to make a living by writing but such freedom was worth any sacrifice until I found out.

I had been toiling happily for a month in my cabin in the woods when a bulky envelope arrived from Springfield, Massachusetts. It contained pamphlets, clippings and a letter from Emerson C. Lowell.

"By now," wrote Mr. Lowell, "you probably think I have forgotten all about my promise to send you more information about the Great Stratemeyer. However, I am not one to forget promises, especially when they deal with important matters and important people. From the capitalized letters you will understand that I have discovered that your friend — and I assume he must be a friend—is a very great man indeed. Not in my world, I am afraid, which is the world of Literature in the higher sense, but in the very peculiar underworld of mass production of reading matter for the young."

Mr. Lowell went on to apologize for his failure to recognize the name of Stratemeyer the moment I made my inquiry. It revealed a lamentable lapse in his knowledge of the American publishing world. It showed that perhaps he had become too deeply absorbed in the output of major publishing houses to spend a little time investigating the substrata of the industry.

This region he found highly fascinating and he thanked me warmly for directing his attention to it.

When Mr. Lowell did a job of research he didn't skimp. He had enclosed a copy of some biographical material on Stratemeyer and a long newspaper clipping about the Great Mathiews-Stratemeyer Feud, which apparently had earned a niche in publishing history.

I read the biographical stuff first and learned that Mr. Stratemeyer began his literary career in Elizabeth, New Jersey, where he penned his first yarn on wrapping paper while waiting counter in his brother's tobacco store. It was traditional, if not downright obligatory, for a novice author in the late eighteen-hundreds to write his first story on brown wrapping paper. This was evidence of poverty and unquenchable determination, both essential to the chosen career. Editors must have been men of healthy eyesight and vast tolerance in those days. Or perhaps they were merely desperate for material. In any case, the editor of *Golden Days*, a boys' magazine in Philadelphia, deciphered the 18,000 words and bought the tale for seventy-five dollars, no doubt accompanying the check with a plaintive request that the new contributor blow some of the money on a pad of white paper.

Encouraged, the young author churned out more stories so rapidly that *Golden Days* couldn't buy them all. He looked around for other markets and found them in *Argosy* and *Golden Argosy*, published by Frank Munsey, whose literary taste was as doubtful as his money-making instinct was certain.

All this success led to the publishing house of Street and Smith in New York City, and a job as editor of a boys' weekly called *Good News*. Stratemeyer was a natural choice for the post. His favorite author had always been Horatio Alger, and he enjoyed writing the same sort of stuff. Stratemeyer not only built up the magazine from a circulation of a few thousand to an astonishing two hundred thousand, but he went on writing.

There is nothing like an editorial job to teach a young writer the facts of life. He learned from the inside. He rid himself of any fancy notions about literature as an art.

Street and Smith was known as the Home of the Dime Novel. It was nothing for Gilbert Patten to turn out a Frank Merriwell story every week. He did it for twenty years under the name of Burt L. Standish. Nor did Frederick Marmaduke Van Renssalear Dey ever flag for an instant while producing his Nick Carter novel every six days for seventeen years. Upton Sinclair could whip up a "True Blue Series" book in a week under his pseudonym of Ensign Clark Fitch, USN.

With these examples to inspire him, young Stratemeyer immediately learned to supplement his income by writing for the "Old Cap Collier Library" under the names Jim Bowie and Nat Woods, whipping out a book a week in addition to his editorial duties. When women's serials were needed for the *New York Weekly*, he underwent a sex change without bothering to go to Denmark and became Julia Edwards, greatly admired by ladies who felt that Julia understood because she was one of them.

Such was life at Street and Smith, where no writer was ever allowed to use his own name, where style was breathless, plots created themselves as one wrote and output was everything. Even if a writer had been exposed to adventures no more exciting than those to be encountered in a tobacco shop or a dusty editorial office, it was expected that he could deliver a Western, a detective story or a rapid-fire tale of adventure in the Himalayas in seven days flat.

As a change of pace, one week Stratemeyer whacked out a serial about a kid on a battleship. He had not, of course, ever been on a battleship. After the serial ran in one of the Street and Smith magazines, Stratemeyer packed it off to Lothrop, Lee and Shepherd in Boston with book publication in mind. He did not know that the firm was on the verge of going broke. Editor Gregory shelved the manuscript because he couldn't afford to print it.

On May 1st, 1898, Admiral Dewey obliterated the Spanish fleet at Manila, which was very big news indeed. Editor Gregory promptly dug out the Stratemeyer script. It had nothing in common with Dewey or Manila except a battleship. Could young Stratemeyer — or whoever he was at the moment — revise the thing a little and make it topical?

To a Street and Smith regular this kind of request was all in the day's work. Stratemeyer could and did. *With Dewey at Manila* hit the bookstores just as the admiral returned for a hero's welcome. It went through so many editions that Lothrop, Lee and Shepherd got out of the red, and was restored to a prosperity it enjoys to the present day.

The Street and Smith experience taught Stratemeyer that when a writer wrote a hit book, he didn't loll around congratulating himself. He got back to work and wrote another just like it. And so the "Old Glory Series" was born and flourished in a climate of patriotic fervor.

Dewey at Manila, a rewritten book which would have sold for a dime in paperback, had made a fortune as a hardcover book at a dollar. Obviously, Stratemeyer decided, the real money was in hardcover juveniles. So he conjured up "The Rover Boys" in 1899 and introduced a couple of new ideas. Normally a juvenile series was content with one hero; but if one hero was good, wouldn't *two* heroes be twice as good? Or even three? As an extra dividend, a lot of dialogue problems would be solved.

He had learned from the "Old Glory" books that a series didn't pick up momentum until several volumes were on the market. This took time. He solved the problem ingeniously. He launched "The Rover Boys" by publishing three books simultaneously: *The Rover Boys at School*, *The Rover Boys at Sea* and *The Rover Boys in the Jungle*. Each book contained a few judicious paragraphs plugging the other two books and each book ended by announcing the title of the book to follow with a hint of the goodies in store. Triple threats of this kind later became known as breeders. They presented the young reader with a full-blown series as a *fait accompli* from the first volume into which he stuck his nose.

"The Rover Boys" sold well enough but failed to rack up the huge sales Stratemeyer expected, even with three heroes and three breeders. He went on turning out more books about the Rover kids while he pondered merchandising ideas. In 1906 he put it all together.

Stratemeyer churned out three breeders for a new series which he called "The Motor Boys." Very few, if any, youngsters were driving their own cars or motorcycles in 1906, but that wasn't the point. All the kids in North America devoutly wished that they *could*. If they had been driving their own cars they would have had neither time nor inclination to read "The Motor Boys" anyway.

Stratemeyer, who had now become Clarence Young, took his fresh set of breeders and a new idea to Cupples and Leon, publishers. The idea was simple. Maybe the one-dollar juvenile was a little steep for kids. How about one for fifty cents, in hardcover? Stratemeyer would be content with a lower royalty if the publishers would be content with a lower profit per book. Volume would do the rest. Look at Frank W. Woolworth!

Cupples and Leon were probably shaken by the experience of meeting an author who actually suggested a royalty cut. Bemused, they examined the proposal.

A hardcover book at fifty cents would have to sell 7,500 copies before it would show a profit. In almost any other line of fiction such a gamble would horrify any publisher who cared to remain solvent, but this was the juvenile field where normal odds didn't apply. They took a look at the scripts Stratemeyer brought along in his briefcase and decided they were breeders of undeniable fertility. Messrs. Cupples and Leon each took a long, deep breath and went for the deal.

They never regretted it. "The Motor Boys" took off like Barney Oldfield.

The magic of the internal combustion engine had a good deal to do with it, of course, but the fifty-cent price actually did the trick! Over the next few years "The Motor Boys" added nineteen new titles, went through thirty-five editions and sold five million copies before they ran out of gas.

"The Motor Boys" had hardly lapped the field before Stratemeyer was over in the Grosset and Dunlap office making a pitch for his lagging "Rover Boys." The fifty-cent price was all the lads needed to goose them into the big money. Grosset and Dunlap, bedazzled by the success of "The Motor Boys," agreed to bring out the Rovers at half a buck.

It was like hitting the motherlode of a gold mine thought to be petering out. At fifty cents, Richard Rover and his brothers found their way into the hands of practically every American youngster who could decipher the printed word.

But it was not as an author alone that Stratemeyer achieved greatness. It was after the death of Horatio Alger, after Stratemeyer had completed a few of the great man's unfinished works, that he conjured up his big idea.

Perhaps he began to wonder when he checked the sales figures. As a mere writer, he had earned a few dollars, but the Alger estate, which owned the outlines and the author's name, had made a lot more. The deal was familiar enough. It was the way these things were done. But wasn't it a little one-sided? Why not reverse the process? Why not concentrate on writing outlines, farm them out to indigent scribblers, then sell the books to publishers?

The notion was epic in its simplicity — one of the great merchandising ideas in the history of American publishing. A stocky, nearsighted, incredibly imaginative man, in his own peculiar field Stratemeyer had the soul of a sales genius.

His great idea was first, to insist on total ownership of the merchandise. Abolish all that royalty nonsense. Writers are always broke — pay them a flat rate, at the lowest possible figure. And never, under any circumstance, permit a writer to sign his own name to a book — that way lies disaster in the shape of future demands for more money. Give the author a pseudonym, make sure to have it copyrighted, and insist on a release of all rights to the manuscript.

Second, show no mercy to any publisher. Make them sweat for every nickel they earn. Cut in on their racket by electroplating the books yourself. Then *lease* — do not sell — the plates.

Third, avoid Alger's deplorable mistake of regarding each

book as an entity. Alger conjured up a new hero every time he sat down to write a book. As a surcease from boredom this was understandable, but it was downright wasteful. *Ragged Dick* sold prodigiously, but think of what Alger could have done with twenty *Ragged Dicks*: *Ragged Dick in the Rockies*! *Ragged Dick in the Desert*! *Ragged Dick on the Midnight Express*! They'd have established sales records that would have staggered even Horatio Alger. Moral — always think in terms of a series. Squeeze the last dime out of a winner.

For Edward Stratemeyer, 1906 was a year that belonged to history because it was the year "The Motor Boys" came roaring out of the pit and the year he established what he called his *Syndicate* in East Orange, New Jersey. Here he went on to father more than a score of series, produce outlines at a prodigious rate for assignment to a platoon of anonymous writers who were forever invisible to each other and to the world, publish 800 books and make himself a million dollars. (Thus fulfilling his mother's prediction when she helped devise his pen name, Arthur M. Winfield: Arthur for Author, Winfield for Winner in the Field, and M, of course, for Million.)

All this was not achieved without opposition. If a man is known by his enemies, Edward Stratemeyer had acquired a foe of considerable eminence and no little ingenuity: Franklin K. Mathiews, chief librarian of the Boy Scouts of America, which had been founded in 1910.

Franklin K. Mathiews was not the sort of man who took *The Rover Boys* in his stride. He felt that parents who merely smiled indulgently when they found their tykes absorbed in the adventures of Richard Rover and his brothers were complacent in the face of perils they didn't recognize. They might as well allow the little fellows to fool around with shotguns assumed to be unloaded.

The Boy Scouts of America had a book division of their own which, under the supervision of Mr. Mathiews, sponsored publications guaranteed to be healthy, entertaining and instructive. Even a very young Boy Scout could learn how to build a camp fire without setting fire to his drawers. He could be instructed in the art of sending useful messages by waving little flags at another Boy Scout at the far end of a field. He could learn how to identify strange animals, birds and reptiles before and after they bit him. He could master the technique of building a tree house and, if he fell out of it, there was a useful volume on first aid which would show him how to set a broken leg.

This, thought good Mr. Mathiews, was the sort of stuff to give the troops. Although several million copies of this lively literature were sold under his auspices, he was dismayed to find that the Boy Scouts of America, to say nothing of a few million unconverted heathen, went right on devouring *The Rover Boys* and even *Tom Swift*, both by the popular author Victor Appleton. When Mr. Mathiews learned that Victor Appleton was none other than his primary foe, Edward Stratemeyer, working under cover, he was not at all surprised. But when he discovered that upward of *twenty* of the more popular series of books aimed at the boys of America were either written or inspired by Stratemeyer, he was appalled. One man, hiding behind more aliases than a bum-check artist, apparently controlled about eighty percent of the books that came into the hands of young America. He dictated not only their style, such as it was, but also their content.

Mr. Mathiews was convinced that the sinister Stratemeyer, if not actually plotting world conquest, was at least well on his way by taking over the minds of American youth.

Indifferent parents, he felt, regarded Stratemeyer's fifty-cent juveniles all too complacently. At the worst they might classify the books, full of frenzied action, as hogwash but harmless in the long run. It was Mr. Mathiew's contention that the hogwash was a bubbling, seething ferment, emanating poisonous fumes which drugged the nation's young into a general state of idiocy.

It was his duty, Mathiews considered, to buckle on the armor of righteousness and go forth to demolish the mastermind while there was yet time. He enlisted a few authors of juvenile fiction, whose work he approved, and went to one of

Stratemeyer's major publishers with a grand proposal by way of counterattack.

The plan was to publish a series of guaranteed, antiseptic "good" books backed by all the resources of the Boy Scouts of America. The campaign would be opened by publication of an article calculated to blast Stratemeyer into oblivion.

The article, first published in a national magazine and later distributed widely as a pamphlet, was called "Blowing Out the Boys' Brains." It came out during Safety First Book Week, another idea dreamed up by Mr. Mathiews as part of his offensive. The article didn't fool around. Mr. Mathiews even likened the Stratemeyer literature to alcohol in its habit-forming and ruinous effects. In fact, he contrived to leave the impression that alcohol, the WCTU notwithstanding, was a lesser evil for the simple reason that few kids ever got hold of the stuff.

Stratemeyer's books, on the other hand, were available at every corner store to every youngster with half a buck in his pocket. Parents and kids alike were warned that the lethal volumes overstimulated the boyish imagination. So doing, they "debauch and vitiate, as brain and body are debauched and destroyed by strong drink."

Mr. Mathiews was no slouch when it came to mounting a nationwide campaign. The Safety First Book Week got a lot of newspaper space when the new series was launched in a blizzard of pamphlets. "Blowing Out the Boys' Brains" was the headliner, of course, but a Safety First booklet explaining how to recognize and cope with brain-blowing literature was issued to every Boy Scout. He was required to read this, probably on pain of being deprived of his toggle.

As Mr. Mathiews was aware, nothing upsets a Boy Scout more than having his toggle lifted.

Thousands of volunteer helpers rallied to the cause. Sound the tocsin of national peril and hordes of well-meaning folk with nothing much to do always materialize from nowhere. They itch to meddle in great matters of which their comprehension is usually pretty dim, and have no objection to getting their names and pictures in the papers. A good organizer can always conjure them up in swarms.

For a while the Stratemeyer products suffered a loss in sales, but only for a while. Eventually, as the volunteers drifted off into other causes (their indignation span being notoriously short), sales recovered. It only proved that you can lead a kid to an approved book but you can't make him read it. Especially if you tell him it is good for him.

The boys knew what they wanted and so did Stratemeyer. He went right on dictating outlines. He even invented several new series. His writers went right on churning out improbable dialogue and more improbable action. The publishers went on printing the hardcover juveniles. The stores replenished their stocks as the half-dollar volumes began moving again and Little Elmer caught up on the *Tom Swifts* he had missed.

I was considerably impressed by these communications from Mr. Lowell. So this was the ghostly group I had joined when I hammered out that first Dave Fearless book! It seemed to me that Edward Stratemeyer was much too modest. Obviously a merchandising and production genius, he belonged right up there with Henry Ford and the Fuller Brush man.

Cheerfully, I fell to work whacking out the day's chapter. I hadn't the faintest intention of resigning from the invisible legion of Stratemeyer's Spooks.

CHAPTER 6:

Enter the Hardy Boys

Now I had come full circle, back to the cabin on the bay, back at the typewriter. There were changes now. I was more experienced. I had become Roy Rockwood, author. The world was still before me.

I finished "The Hill of Gold" in 25,000 words and sent it off to *Adventure* with great confidence. I also finished *Dave Fearless Near the South Pole* and sent it off to the Syndicate in a mildly disturbed state of mind. This was because the final paragraph of the outline failed to include the usual plug for an upcoming volume. There was no hint of a title for a sequel.

As a result, Dave's adventures in the Antarctic ended on a pretty flat note. As the ship headed homeward with Lem and Bart Hankers in irons down below, Dave Fearless said, "A successful voyage after all," to which Bob replied with characteristically ready wit, "I'll say it was." Author Rockwood, for his part, could dredge up nothing better than "On and on sailed the good ship *Swallow* and here we will leave Dave Fearless and say goodbye." It had the alarming aspects of a permanent farewell, not only to Dave Fearless and friend but to further assignments from the Stratemeyer Syndicate.

I fretted for a couple of weeks. Perhaps I had killed Dave Fearless by bad writing. On sober consideration, however, I knew this was impossible. Only if the books took to using four-syllable words would Dave's admirers ever abandon him for reasons having to do with the quality of the prose. It was more reasonable to suppose that Mr. Stratemeyer had merely run out of geography.

Shortly thereafter, a letter came from Arthur Hoffman. He was sorry, he said, but "Hill of Gold" had been read with interest and he agreed with his editors that it wasn't an *Adventure* story. Just what was meant by that he didn't explain. However, he had taken the liberty to "send it down the hall" to another magazine in the Butterick establishment. It left a thin ray of hope, but I expected the worst.

Every freelance fiction writer has, at one time or another, empathized with Eliza of *Uncle Tom's Cabin*. As she stumbles across the Ohio River on treacherous ice floes that keep shifting or breaking underfoot, carrying a tot in her arms, with a cataract ahead of her and bloodhounds behind her, the safety of the distant shore highly in doubt, the freelance knows exactly how she felt.

By the end of summer half a dozen stories that once looked like reliable ice floes had turned into rejection slips that wouldn't support the weight of a flea. The cheerful assumption that Dave Fearless would keep me afloat while I leaped nimbly toward the solvency represented by the approval of magazine editors who paid real money had vanished in the blizzard of little printed notes that expressed regrets and assured me that no lack of merit was implied. The butcher, the grocer and the man who sold beer weren't exactly baying for my blood but they were making discouraging noises.

In short, I was damn near broke. There was no comfort in recalling that Eliza had made it, even encumbered by a babe in arms. Eliza had existed only in the imagination of Harriet Beecher Stowe, who controlled the ice floes and saw to it that the bloodhounds didn't gain on her. This was real.

It has since occurred to me that there is an easy explanation for the fact that some writers always seem to be involved in hideous difficulties. They mismanage their lives and wives; they court cirrhosis with happy abandon; they go on expense-paid hegiras to Las Vegas; they invest their money in schemes that even a bumpkin at a country fair would recognize as so palpably larcenous that he would clap his hand on his wallet and yell for the police. They elope with adenoidal broads they meet in massage parlors. There is simply no end to the imaginative methods they can find to ensure total personal disaster, to see to it that outrageous fortune will clobber them with slings and arrows to the end of their days.

Why? They merely become incapable of distinguishing between fact and fiction. Because ingenuity never fails them when it comes to extricating some character from a fearsome dilemma, they embark on the most addlepated enterprises, armed with confidence that the same ingenuity can be counted on to rescue them from equally fearsome mishaps of their own devising.

Invariably they are flabbergasted when it doesn't work, when they discover that in life the missing will seldom turns up, the couple who thought they would live happily ever after often begin clawing at each other within a few days of the ceremony, the murderer frequently goes his jolly way, undetected, and the midnight bell occasionally strikes exactly sixty minutes after the eleventh-hour rescue has failed to materialize on schedule.

This time, however, my faith in the world as it should be was happily confirmed. Just as the wagon train was about to go up in smoke, the troops came clattering over the hill with flags flying and bugles blaring. Mr. Oscar Graeve, discerning editor of a reputable magazine called *Everybody's*, wrote to the effect that he thought my story about the old prospector was pretty good and enclosed a check for $500. My shaky line of credit with the butcher and the grocer was restored; the man who sold beer was happy to let me have a few cases. But more important, however, was that a point had apparently been made. Can a young man of unproven talents, living in the northern Ontario woods, finance a career in authorship? Definitely, he could. For a few months anyway.

I was tempted then to write Edward Stratemeyer a letter of resignation. Something wryly humorous. But final. Something like this:

Dear Ed:
(That would startle him. Up to now our communications had been on a formal plane.)

I am afraid Dave and I just don't get along. Nothing personal, mind. His moral character is impeccable. His courage in the face of impending disaster cannot be questioned. I have conducted him through Arctic wastes and tropical jungles, in and out of the damnedest perils ever conceived by the mind of man. But dim-witted bravery is not enough. Fearless has the mind of a cretin; in fact, he is such a dull, insufferable bastard that I can't stand him any longer. This also goes for his creepy pal, Vilett, that phony old Captain Broadbeam and that stage Irishman, Pat Stoodles. As for Lem and Bart Hankers, those fumble-handed idiots, while deploring their ineptitude in villainy I can at least sympathize with their persistent efforts to rid the world of the obnoxious Fearless-Vilett team.

As it seems highly improbable that this will ever happen, I feel that I have reached the end of my endurance and that I can only preserve my sanity by getting clear of the whole grisly business. Don't send me any more Dave Fearless outlines, for the love of God.

Yours, rebelliously,
Roy Rockwood (ret.)

This communication was already in draft when native caution intervened. Maybe Oscar Graeve wouldn't send me a $500 check for another story. What if this happened to be a temporary lull in the storm, with another blizzard of rejection slips hovering just over the horizon?

Under these circumstances a guaranteed $100 check each month was certainly not to be sneezed at, even at the cost of enduring the witless society of Dave Fearless, Bob Vilett, Captain Broadbeam, the Hankers and even the intolerable Pat Stoodles a while longer. Perhaps I had better wait.

Furthermore, a letter from Stratemeyer came a few days' later. This time no new outline was attached. Instead, he announced that he had "other plans." While he didn't come right out and say so, I gathered that readers had come to share my weariness with the underwater adventurers. This should have cheered me. It didn't. It was one thing for me to abandon Dave Fearless, quite another thing for Dave Fearless to abandon me. I felt basely betrayed.

For three days I moped around the cabin trying to conjure up an idea for a story that might please Oscar Graeve. Ideas came but each was hastily rejected as too risky. Self-confidence, the stock-in-trade of the freelance writer, had disappeared. I kept recalling a couple of lines that ended a critical chapter in *Dave Fearless on The Lost Brig*.

> *Dave's heart sank into his diving boots when he realized*
> *what had happened. The Hankers had cut his air hose!*
> *"Steady, boy!" he told himself. "This is no time to*
> *panic."*

This example of calmness in the face of disaster didn't really help. It was all very well for Dave Fearless to meet catastrophe with aplomb. *He* could count on Bob Vilett and Captain Broadbeam to haul him to the surface, while Pat Stoodles lent encouragement by bellowing "Heave-ho, bejabers!" I couldn't count on anyone — except, perhaps, Edward Stratemeyer.

It turned out that I *could* count on Edward Stratemeyer. Before the week was out a long envelope brought another outline, accompanied by a letter explaining his "other plans." He had observed, Stratemeyer wrote, that detective stories had become very popular in the world of adult fiction. He instanced the works of S.S. Van Dine, which were selling in prodigious numbers as I was well aware. S.S. Van Dine was neither an ocean liner nor a living man but the pseudonym of Willard Hungtington Wright, a literary craftsman who wrote sophisticated stories for Mencken's *Smart Set*.

It had recently occurred to him, Stratemeyer continued, that the growing boys of America might welcome similar fare. Of course, he had already given them Nat Ridley, but Nat really didn't solve mysteries; he merely blundered into them and, after a given quota of hairbreadth escapes, blundered out again. What Stratemeyer had in mind was a series of detective stories on the juvenile level, involving two brothers of high-school age who would solve such mysteries as came their way. To lend credibility to their talents, they would be the sons of a professional private investigator, so big in his field that he had become a sleuth of international fame. His name — Fenton Hardy. His sons, Frank and Joe, would therefore be known as . . .

The Hardy Boys!

This would be the title of the series. My pseudonym would be Franklin W. Dixon. (I never did learn what the "W" represented. Certainly not Wealthy.)

Stratemeyer noted that the books would be clothbound and therefore priced a little higher than paperbacks. This in turn would justify a little higher payment for the manuscript— $125 to be exact. He had attached an information sheet for guidance and the plot outline of the initial volume, which would be called *The Tower Treasure*. In closing, he promised that if the manuscript came up to expectations — which were high — I would be asked to do the next two volumes of the series.

The background information was terse. The setting would be a small city called Bayport on Barmet Bay "somewhere on the Atlantic Coast." The boys would attend Bayport High. Their mother's name would be Laura. They would have three chums: Chet, a chubby farm boy, humorist of the group; Biff Hooper, an athletic two-fisted type who could be relied on to balance the scales in the event of a fight; and Tony Prito, who would presumably tag along to repesent all ethnic minorities.

Two girls would also make occasional appearances. One of them, Iola Morton, sister of Chet, would be favorably regarded by Joe. The Other, Callie Shaw, would be tolerated by Frank. It was intimated that relations between the Hardy boys and their girl friends would not go beyond the borders of wholesome friendship and discreet mutual esteem.

I got the message. There was to be no petting, as it was known at the time. None of the knee-pawing, tit-squeezing stuff that was sneaking in to so much popular fiction, to the disgust of all right-thinking people. Wholesome American boys never got a hard-on. (Why was that?)

I skimmed through the outline. It was about a robbery in a towered mansion belonging to Hurd Applegate, an eccentric stamp collector. The Hardy Boys solved it.

What a change from Dave Fearless! No man-eating sharks. No octopi. No cannibals, polar bears or man-eating trees. Just the everyday doings of everyday lads in everyday surroundings. They didn't go wandering all over the seven seas, pursued by imbecile relatives. They stayed at home, checked in for dinner every night like other kids. They even went to school. Granted, they didn't appear to spend very much time at school; most of the outline seemed to be devoted to extracurricular activities after four and on weekends. But they went.

I was so relieved to be free of Dave Fearless and his dreary helpers that I greeted Frank and Joe Hardy with positive rapture, and I wrote to Stratemeyer to accept the assignment. Then I rolled a sheet of paper into the typewriter and prepared to go to work.

Then I paused and gave the project a little thought. The sensible course would have been to hammer out the thing at breakneck speed, regardless of style, spelling or grammar, and let the Stratemeyer editors tidy it up. Bang it out, stuff the typed sheets in an envelope and put it in the mail, the quicker the better, and get going on the next book. In this sort of business, at the payment involved, time was money, output was everything.

Writers, however, aren't always sensible. Many of them enjoy writing so much that they would go on doing it even if deprived of bylines and checks, which is why agents are born. The enjoyment implies doing the best one can with the task in hand, even if it is merely an explanatory letter to the landlord. (There is no special virtue in this. Writers just can't help it.)

It seemed to me that the Hardy boys deserved something better than the slapdash treatment Dave Fearless had been getting. It was still hack work, no doubt, but did the new series have to be all that hack? There was, after all, the chance to contribute a little style, occasional words of more than two syllables, maybe a little sensory stimuli.

Take food, for example. From my boyhood reading I recalled enjoying any scenes that involved eating. Boys are always hungry. Whether the outline called for it or not, I decided that the Hardy boys and their chums would eat frequently. When Laura Hardy packed a picnic lunch the provender would be described in detail, not only when she stowed it away but when the boys did. And when the boys solved the mystery of the theft, Hurd Applegate wouldn't stop at a mere cash reward. He would come up with a lavish dinner, good for at least two pages of lip smacking. Maybe even belches.

And then there was humor. There hadn't been so much as a snicker in the whole Dave Fearless series. This stood to reason: a man-eating shark is no laughing matter. Next to food, however, boys like jokes. Why not inject a few rib ticklers into *The Tower Treasure*? Chet Morton was described as a "fun loving lad," and, as he was supposed to be "chubby," it followed that food interest might be maintained by making him a glutton. The cast of characters also gave passing mention to Chief Collig, head of the Bayport Police Department, and his associate, Detective Smuff. While the outline did not suggest that these lawmen were comical fellows, it did seem that anyone named Collig had to be a pretty stodgy cop and that Smuff would simply have to be a dunderhead.

I could hardly wait to get at them.

But why go to all this trouble? If *The Tower Treasure* was a little better written than the usual fifty-cent juvenile, who would get the credit? The nonexistent Franklin W. Dixon. If better writing and a little humor helped make the series a success, who would benefit financially? The Stratemeyer Syndicate and the publishers. The writer who brought the skeleton outline to life wouldn't get a penny even if the books sold a million — which, of course, seemed impossible at the time.

So what? I decided against the course of common sense. I opted for Quality.

CHAPTER 7:

The Tower Treasure
(For Starters)

The typewriter clattered: "Chapter One: The Speed Demon."

As the boys jounced noisily on their way to the village of Willowville they discussed their mutual ambition to follow in the footsteps of their father, Fenton Hardy, internationally famous private sleuth. The whole passage of dialogue, improbably conducted over the racket of two motorcycles, depressed me. I put an end to it as quickly as possible and moved into the heavy action: the lads were being overtaken by an automobile apparently driven by a maniac. Normally the situation would merely call for evasive action (taking to the shoulder), but a normal situation wouldn't do, as any old hand from the pulp diggings knows. It is necessary to arrange the topography so that an abnormal situation will prevail.

I decided to conjure up a very steep cliff towering above the road on the left and balance it with a very steep declivity dropping off precipitously on the right, straight down into the waters of Barmet Bay. Without a shoulder for refuge, the situation now contained the essential elements of peril, as the pursuing car and lunatic-in-charge gained rapidly on the Hardy boys.

They looked back again. The car was being driven so recklessly that it bounced all over the road, weaving from side to side. It lurched toward the cliff in a cloud of dust. It veered to the other side of the road and almost took off into the sea. The

Hardy boys decided to pull over to the shoulder only to find —
thanks to my topographical arrangements — that it had been
replaced by a 200-foot drop to Barmet Bay, straight down, as
the skidding car hurtled right at them.

End of Chapter One.

There may have been some readers who broke into a cold
sweat at this stage and couldn't wait to read Chapter Two to
find out if the lads met instant death. If so, they were very
young, deplorably naive or perhaps a little backward. Before
they finished *The Tower Treasure* they would have learned the
main fact of life in the world of juvenile fiction: no peril, no
danger, no catastrophe, however grim and apparently ines-
capable, is ever as bad as it seems. These innocents were no
doubt vastly relieved when the car missed the boys by inches in
the second paragraph of Chapter Two and went bounding and
skidding on its errant way.

But not before a clue was planted. The boys saw that the
driver of the car had "a shock of red hair." On the way to
Willowville they discovered a wrecked car, minus license
plates, in the ditch. After checking, like good citizens, to make
sure no one was pinned in the wreckage, they went on to Chet
Morton's place, "a big, homelike, rambling old farmhouse with
an apple orchard at the rear."

This apple orchard was important as a source of provender
for the amiable Chet. Whenever he appeared in a Hardy Boys
book, from that day onward it was invariably noted that he was
eating an apple, which established him as a bit of a glutton. He
gobbled up the produce of the whole orchard every year.

The boys found their chum, Chet, in a wrathful mood.
Some scamp had just stolen his brand-new, yellow roadster.
Tally-ho! All three boys piled onto the Hardy motorcycles and
roared away in search of the thief. First, however, they paid
another visit to the wrecked car in the ditch where the Hardy
boys discovered something they had unaccountably failed to
notice the first time: this was the very car that had nearly
bounced them into Barmet Bay. They figured it all out in a jiffy:

the red-haired speed demon, after coming to grief in the ditch, had pinched Chet's car.

Tally-ho again, pausing only once to make inquiries along the way. This gave me a great opportunity to work in a little comedy by way of some over-the-fence dialogue with four rustics toiling in a field. These yokels were so obtuse that they debated solemnly the issue of whether the car that had recently gone by was a roadster or a delivery truck. Then they engaged in a wild argument over the respective merits of touring cars and coupes, reaching the brink of combat, when the boys departed unenlightened.

A real knee-slapper, that passage, with its not-so-subtle reflections on the mentality of the agricultural community. In the 1920s, stereotypes in humor were predictable: Negroes were always cowardly, shiftless, lazy and unlettered; Irishmen were incredibly dumb; Jews were avaricious; Scots were stingy; farmers — otherwise known as hayseeds — were credulous idiots. A smart-ass comedian never wanted for targets.

About two pages later, when the boys reached Bayport and headed for the police station to report the theft of Chet's car, I had another goldplated opportunity to exercise my comic itch. Cops were always good for laughs. And here were two of them — Chief Collig and Detective Smuff.

Chorting happily, I typed my way through a rib-tickling encounter between the boys and two of the dumbest cops I could dream up. That scene, I told myself with pardonable pride, could be guaranteed to send every kid lucky enough to read it into hysterics. A belly-buster.

It never occurred to me that these scenes could be construed as subversive, that educators and librarians — mighty sour folk at any time—might scream that my belly-buster was deliberately calculated to shatter any respect the kids might have for the sacred institutions of law and order. I wasn't writing for educators and librarians; I was writing for youngsters.

In any case, the big comedy scene was interrupted by the

arrival of Ike Harrity, ticket seller at the steamboat office, reporting a hold-up, and a witness who said the hold-up man had driven away in a yellow roadster and that the fellow was redheaded. The only trouble was that Harrity had described the man as dark haired.

When great confusion and argument ensued, the Hardy boys went home to consult their father. The internationally famous detective wasn't very helpful, although he gave them a lecture to the effect that a good detective must be very observant and pay attention to details. As an object lesson he embarrassed them by asking them the color of the school superintendent's hair. Joe said it was brown; Frank said it was black.

Fenton Hardy, who had seen the superintendent only once in his life while crossing a street, humbled his sons by informing them that the superintendent was bald and wore a chestnut wig. He added that the pedagogue wore buttoned shoes, was a member of the Elks and a great fan of the late Charles Dickens. He had learned these facts in five seconds flat, by one observant look. All this was straight out of Sherlock Holmes. In fact, Sherlock would probably have muffed the elk's tooth clue and wondered, instead, why superintendent Norton was wearing a lousy tooth as a watch-charm on his waistcoat.

It was not until Chapter Seven, however, that the book got into high gear when Hurd Applegate, an eccentric philatelist who lived with his sister, Adelia, in the Tower Mansion on the outskirts of Bayport, was robbed of $40,000 worth of jewels and securities. Understandably, he had so little confidence in the Bayport police force with its assorted stumblebums that he took his troubles to Fenton Hardy.

First, however, he fired his caretaker, Henry Robinson. It appeared that honest Henry had just paid off a $900 bank loan. This automatically made him a suspect character. As a result young Perry Robinson, school chum of the Hardy boys and therefore an upright lad of high moral character, had to leave school and go to work in a grocery store to support the family. As a further consequence, the Robinsons were kicked out of their living quarters in the Tower Mansion and forced to set up housekeeping in "a poor quarter of the city." (Bayport wasn't rich enough to afford slums.)

The sad situation now provided material for an affecting scene in which Frank and his girl friend, Callie Shaw, went to visit the afflicted family. Clearly, Henry Robinson was unjustly accused. Out of work, he was also ineligible for unemployment benefits, welfare or food stamps because the Coolidge administration hadn't created these benefits. Frank and Callie were touched by Mrs. Robinson's gallant efforts to keep the humble cottage clean and neat, as well as by her faith in husband Henry's innocence. The fact that this lachrymose chapter was based on practically every book Horatio Alger ever wrote didn't bother me a bit.

Fenton Hardy latched onto a clue and disappeared on the trail of a rascal named Red Jackley, an ex-con with a weakness for burglary and red wigs. Red Jackley was now lying unconscious and on the point of death in an out-of-town hospital, and might recover just long enough to make a death-bed confession.

Then the Bayport Keystone Kops showed up. They too had heard about Jackley and now declared themselves in on any death-bed confessions that might be floating around. Clearly, if Fenton Hardy was to claim credit and reward, somebody had to prevent Chief Collig and Detective Smuff from boarding the seven o'clock train. This problem paved the way for one of my great comic set pieces — the Great Fruit Stand Bomb Hoax — established on the shaky premises that all cops are dumb and that any immigrant who hasn't mastered the English language is just naturally an object of mirth.

It was Chet Morton's idea to plant a bomb in the fruit stand of Rocco, a character of infinite humorous possibilities because he tacked an "a" to the end of every verb, was highly excitable and had a very silly fear of the Black Hand organization, the 1926 forerunner of the Mafia. The bomb, of course, was merely an alarm clock in a shoebox, but when the Hardy boys and their merry chums called Rocco's attention to the ticking noise and suggested that Rocco had incurred the enmity of the Black Hand, instant comedy erupted. The frantic Rocco danced in the street, shrieking his apprehensions in splintered English and yelling for the police. Chief Collig and Detective Smuff lumbered to the scene, all bluster and bravery until they heard the oranges ticking away, whereupon they dissolved into abject cowardice. Now, to their relief, an even more comic member of the Bayport constabulary came plodding around the corner in the person of Constable Con Riley, who was promptly ordered to locate and dispose of the bomb.

Over the years, dozens of small boys have told me that the Bomb Hoax has always been high on their private list of Select Comic Readings of All Time. Snickering, they recalled their glee when Con Riley poured about forty buckets of water on the fruit stand, quaking while Collig and Smuff urged him from a safe distance and promised him a staff funeral if the oranges blew up. Grown men have assured me that they still remember the scene with affection.

In any event, the Hoax served a double purpose. It made the kids laugh and it made Collig and Smuff miss their train.

Fenton Hardy was the only person at Jackley's bedside when the criminal rallied long enough to confess that the loot was hidden "in the old tower."

At this point it appeared that the case was all wrapped up. All the Hardy boys had to do now was search the towers of Hurd Applegate's mansion and recover the gems and securities. Then they could pocket the reward and go around town taking well-earned bows. But this was merely the end of Chapter Sixteen. With eight more chapters to go, any reasonably bright reader would understand that it wasn't going to be all that easy, And it wasn't.

When the Hardy boys ransacked the towers, they drew a blank. Hurd Applegate and Sister Adelia threw them out. Fenton Hardy was "dumbfounded." Even Con Riley subjected the lads to public ridicule when he caught up with them on a downtown corner. Mr. Robinson, instead of being cleared by Red Jackley's confession, was arrested all over again as an accomplice. Son Perry, instead of showing up at Bayport High on Monday morning, checked back in at the grocery store. Mrs.

Robinson canceled the order for the moving van, reviewed her recipes for hamburg and scrubbed the floor of the humble abode all over again. As for Collig and Smuff, they laughed and laughed.

However, it all turned out fine by Chapter Twenty-four.

For the benefit of any who have unaccountably forgotten the denouement that delighted them so many years ago, they need only be reminded that Frank and Joe came up with a brilliant feat of deduction. They directed their search toward an abandoned water tower by the railway tracks. ("In the old tower." Get it?) There they found the loot, right where Jackley had hidden it. Every gem and every bond.

Chapter Twenty-four wrote itself: Henry Robinson got out of jail again, this time for keeps; Chief Collig bawled out Detective Smuff for stupidity; Perry Robinson resigned from the grocery store and went back to school; the Robinson family returned to their old quarters in the Tower Mansion; and Hurd Applegate forked over a reward of $1,000, which was mighty good money for those days (readers even heard his pen scratching as he wrote two $500 checks for the Hardy boys).

Then he invited the lads and their chums to dinner.

At least that's what the outline indicated. Just dinner. But why skimp? What Franklin W. Dixon provided was a banquet, a feast. He saw to it that young readers savored the sight, smell and taste of roast chicken "crisp and brown" with huge helpings of mashed potatoes and gravy. He served them pickles, vegetables and salads. He encouraged seconds. And when it came to dessert, he didn't take the easy way out and settle for a couple of cartons of ice cream. He whomped up half a dozen kinds of pie *with* ice cream.

Young readers learned then and there that when it came to food, Franklin W. was not a man to count the cost. No cheapskate, he. At one stage he lost his head completely and even allowed the lads to put their elbows on the table. Millions of dismayed mothers probably wondered about the national decline in juvenile table manners which swept the nation in 1927 and subsequent years. Now they know.

After a few pages of loose-ends cleanup, *The Tower Treasure* was finished, and off to East Orange, New Jersey.

Awaiting Stratemeyer's verdict, I tried to redeem my soul by writing a somber tale about a northern Ontario settler and his wife who took refuge in an underground root cellar during a forest fire. They spent most of the time yelling at each other and gasping for breath. Heavy stuff. No banquet for them when they got out, although there was plenty of roast chicken lying around.

Weeks later, a fat envelope came from Stratemeyer. It contained outlines for two more Hardy boys books: *The House on the Cliff* and *The Secret of the Old Mill*. There was also a letter, a check and a document that looked vaguely legal. The document, a contract, was very simple — it covered everything. It was a release form absolving me of any rights to any volumes already written or any that might be written in the future for the Stratemeyer Syndicate. It covered the plots, the titles, the Roy Rockwood name, the name of Franklin W. Dixon and the manuscripts, forever and ever. Furthermore, it included a promise that I would never under any circumstances divulge to anyone the fact that I had ever written a Dave Fearless book or a Hardy Boys book under any title or pen name for anyone.

The penalty for such a revelation wasn't spelled out. I assumed that it had something to do with boiling in oil.

I had no hesitation in signing this document. As a matter of fact, I had been doing a little thinking about the matter. The release saved me the trouble of asking Stratemeyer to do me a similar favor. No sworn affidavits — merely his signature to a promise that he would never tell anyone I ever wrote books for him.

I was glad we understood each other.

Then I turned to the letter, which acknowledged and paid for *The Tower Treasure*. As usual, Edward Stratemeyer managed to keep his emotions well under control. If he thought *The Tower Treasure* was great stuff, jam packed with humor and suspense, he was able to curb any expression of his enthusiasm. Maybe he thought an order for two more books spoke for itself. Perhaps I should have regarded it as the equivalent of an unrestrained burst of applause, but I didn't.

I thought that I had written a hell of a good book — of its kind — and that it rated at least a line of favorable comment. Surely Stratemeyer, being an author himself, realized that writers do not live by bread alone, that without praise they perish. Then it occurred to me that Stratemeyer, of course, regarded *The Tower Treasure* as *his* book and that it would be indecorous of him to come right out and say it was a lallapaloosa. Even so, he didn't have to be all that modest.

Accustomed to the commercial plugs that adorned opening and closing chapters of the Dave Fearless saga, I was prepared for his instructions about the advertising matter I would have to weave cunningly into the texture of my prose.

As for the obligatory plug for Volume Four, Stratemeyer was uncommunicative. This disappointed me. I was curious about the title of Number Four, which suggested that I was getting hooked myself.

Then I recalled my letter from Mr. Lowell, and everything became clear. The three books were breeders. Stratemeyer was launching the Hardy Boys in the same way he had launched his immortal Rovers, with a triple-barrel blast. The three books would be published simultaneously. A kid who read one book would be tempted to read the others. Edward Stratemeyer and the publisher—whoever *he* turned out to be—would bide their time and wait for the sales report. Then, and only then, would there be a decision about Volume Four. After that, with any luck at all, Volume Five would be added in a sort of snowball effect, rolling on and on, the series accumulating more and more readers. Perhaps there might be a Volume Ten. My imagination stopped there.

This merely proves that I wasn't Thinking Big. That there would be a Volume Sixty nearly half a century later was quite beyond my power of fancy. Imagination is fine but you've got to keep it within limits. There is such a thing as being ridiculous.

I rolled a sheet of paper into the typewriter, flattened the first page of the outline of *The House on the Cliff* on the table and pondered. Now then. What was going to happen in Chapter One?

Reminiscent of the first chapter of *The Tower Treasure*, it was again a Saturday, again the Hardy boys were on their motorcycles and again they were riding along the Shore Road. This time Chet Morton was with them because he too had acquired a motorcycle. Again there was a good deal of dialogue of an expository nature, most of it concerning events that had occurred at the Tower Mansion. A discerning reader might have wondered why the lads had to keep reminding each other.

The subsequent plot also involved an unusual dwelling. This time it was a haunted house, called the Old Polucca Place. When I came across this in the outline, it struck me as an interesting departure for Stratemeyer. A home for retired prizefighters offered genuine possibilities. It turned out, how-ever, that the Old Polucca Place was merely a ramshackle building that was said to be haunted. It sheltered a gang of dope smugglers led by a rascal named Red Snackley.

Red Snackley?

Right on the heels of the late Red Jackley? Stratemeyer was in a rut. He was, obviously, prejudiced against redheads. I entertained myself with a plausible explanation, going way back to some distant afternoon in Elizabeth, New Jersey, when young Stratemeyer had an afternoon off from the cigar store and plunked down a hard-earned half dollar to see a vaudeville show. There he suffered through an act so dreadful that he had never forgotten it.

JACKLEY & SNACKLEY
Those Redheaded Rascals
Songs, Dances and Patter

They wore striped jackets and carried canes. They grinned incessantly. They sang off key. Between choruses, Jackley asked Snackley why a fireman wore red suspenders. Jackley asked if he knew the difference between an old maid and a watermelon. They were awful and Stratemeyer hated them. Now, years later, he was having his revenge.

By this time I had become an old pro, capable of hammering out a chapter in less than half an hour if all the characters talked a lot. Dialogue wrote itself. Exposition and action took longer.

Once again Fenton Hardy disappeared for several chapters. This time his sons got worried and went looking for him. They had help from a truck driver named Sam Bates, who told of having seen the great detective near the Old Polucca Place. Sam was almost a comic character. He talked so slowly and rambled so extensively that his account was good for a whole chapter. More comedy came in when the Hardy boys passed the information along to Chief Collig and Detective Smuff, while those lawmen were playing a game of checkers, and tried to needle them into action.

As usual, it was up to the Hardy boys. A dangerous voyage by motor boat, the discovery of a cave full of smuggled goods, the revelation that Fenton Hardy was held prisoner and that his captor was none other than the infamous Red Snackley and "the worst fears of the Hardy boys were realized."

In the end, of course, the Hardy boys overcame, a grateful government dished out the usual thousand dollars reward and the boys spent some of the money entertaining their chums at a dinner that eclipsed even the feast at the end of *The Tower Treasure*.

I wrote a deft paragraph suggesting that young readers keep their eyes peeled for the next volume of the series, to be called *The Secret of the Old Mill*, before I whacked out "The End" and thrust the pages into an envelope.

I got into the canoe and paddled three miles up the lake, bound for the Sudbury post office. It was a bleak journey. It was autumn and the leaves were gone, the islands were harsh in outline, big waves splashed over the bow. Gales and snow squalls were in the air.

Back in the cabin that night, with the bare trees thrashing, sleet splattering on the roof, I knew it was time to close up the place before winter came. I had even begun to hear voices in the big waves that crashed on the beach. One could never make out exactly what the voices were saying but tonight their message was clear enough: *Get going!*

CHAPTER 8:

Home-town Boy Returns

In small-town communities it is generally assumed that if a home-town boy comes back for more than a brief round of handshakes he has failed to Make Good. Somehow, he has blown it in the outside world. If he remains he is of interest only as visible evidence of the superior wisdom of the natives who stayed put.

So it was that when I returned to Haileybury, moved back in with my parents and brothers, rented an office above a bank and set up shop as author-in-residence, no one was visibly impressed. Perhaps it was because no one had ever heard of Dave Fearless.

In the forty-seven years since then, in fact, I have never encountered anyone who has heard of Dave Fearless. I have never seen a Dave Fearless book in a bookstore, on a paperback rack, on a library shelf or even in any of the dusty caves in obscure shops where old books go when they die. I have never come across any reference to Dave in any book or article. On a shelf in my small library the yellowing volumes I hammered out for Edward Stratemeyer stand as the solid evidence that there actually was a Dave Fearless series. Otherwise I might begin to doubt.

It is improbable that they are listed anywhere except in the files of the Garden City Publishing Company. There will be copies, of course, in the Library of Congress in Washington as well as in that incredible library stored in the offices of the Stratemeyer Syndicate, now in Maplewood, New Jersey — that library of more than 800 books all written or inspired by the Great Edward.

A scholar in the future may decipher one and write a learned essay on Literary Tastes of the Early Twentieth Century. From this rare and therefore precious specimen of Americana, he may even draw interesting conclusions about Roy Rockwood, Primitive Apostle of Escapism. He may note that the career of this author is steeped in mystery, that biographical references have been lost, that date and place of birth are unknown to literary historians.

Otherwise — oblivion.

Q: Did Dave Fearless deserve oblivion?

A: Damn right.

I didn't even mention the Hardy Boys in Haileybury, except to my mother, because I was at an age when one is easily intimidated by any document that looks legal. I had taken very seriously that contract which enjoined me to secrecy about my labors for the Syndicate and which made me subject to unmentionable penalties if I blabbed. Unmentionable because they weren't mentioned, which made them all the more sinister. So I nursed my guilty secret and went on nursing it, in fact, for many years after anyone had stopped caring.

Haileybury will always be my home town. I first saw the place in 1910 when I was a kid of eight. The place had begun as a settlement in the bush but by the time my family moved there it had grown into a big town by northern Ontario standards, with plank sidewalks and a lot of mud. It also had a modern public school, of which my father was the new principal and thus a citizen of the first rank. Even in its primitive days Haileybury was a lovely town because it was built on a sloping hillside overlooking a majestic lake called Temiskaming. Seven miles in width, it was actually an enlargement of the Ottawa River, the natural boundary between the provinces of Ontario and Quebec.

Although it was the place where I grew up, it was no

longer the home town I remembered. Northen Ontario is subject to bushfires and one October afternoon in 1922 a holocaust had turned the pleasant hillside into a black heap of rubble. The town had been rebuilt and most of the landmarks of boyhood had vanished. But I insisted on recalling the town that used to be, a rowdy town, a pioneer town. And strangely, because it was so familiar, I had seldom used it as a background for fiction nor could I see its people as characters in stories. They were too real, too vivid in memory.

The lake was the enduring element that gave Haileybury its character. Not only did it convey a majestic sense of spaciousness, but it was infinite with change. Its mood would vary with the seasons, the weather, even with the time of day. On fine mornings in the summer it lay glassy and still with a shimmer on the water under a cloudless sky. When clouds gathered and there was a tossing of whitecaps, you could see the rain coming down from the north. You could watch its progress as it obscured the headlands and islands, as it blotted out the distant Quebec shore and came sweeping southward in great sheets over the waves rolling before the wind. In winter it was a vast expanse of white snow, acres of purity in a light so clear that even the small dwellings on the other shore were sharply defined. When the snowstorms came they advanced with white banners flying in an onrush of dancing flakes that softly enclosed our world.

The citizens in that early day were a little touchy to any suggestion that Haileybury was a community that owed its eminence to liquor. They said that this was a base canard invented by envious natives of less enterprising places in the outlands. Unfortunately, there was more than a grain of truth in the charge.

Five miles to the south was the mining town of Cobalt, center of the Cobalt silver camp, famed for the great Silver Stampede of 1904 which drew hordes of miners, prospectors, promoters, speculators and incidental riffraff from all over the world. All money-hungry. All booze-thirsty. The provincial lawmakers, mindful of the skulduggery and bloodshed that made the mining camps of Nevada and the Klondike synonymous with Sodom and Gomorrah, decreed that no liquor could be sold within five miles of any mining camp in Ontario. This was a matter of concern to the silver seekers until it was learned that the bush community of Haileybury was exactly five miles from Cobalt and thus provided a legal oasis. Several oases, in fact: four great roaring hotels and a liquor store.

The hotels were none of your green-lumber-and-tarpaper affairs either. They featured solid brick and stone masonry, comfortable bedrooms, indoor johns, dining rooms with real tablecloths and bathrooms. Even the names of the hotels had character. In stodgier communities to the south the names of hotels always paid deference to the Royal Family. You had the Queen Victoria, the King Edward, the Prince George, or maybe just the Queen's. This would be enough for the average town although with expansion there might be a Windsor or a Royal, but not in Haileybury. Our clientele was cosmopolitan and many of the customers who bellied up to the bar owed their allegiance to the Stars and Stripes and were a little baffled by all this homage to royalty overseas. Haileybury hotel owners were a liberated lot, given to originality, and so we had the Matabanick (an Indian word meaning "the place where you come out"), the Maple Leaf (a Canadian symbol), the Vendome (a continental touch) and the Attorney (for some obscure reason). Each had its own polished mahogany bar with impeccable mirrors, shelves of gleaming glassware, beer pumps, rows and rows of bottles with gaudy labels and aphrodisiacal paintings in gilt frames. Genuine works of art depicting alluring girls with big tits, languishing on sofas in postures of surrender and wearing not a stitch.

Man! Those were bars!

This does not mean that Haileybury became a drunkards' paradise. After all, in a climate where winters are long and the temperature is known to drop beneath forty below zero, liquor is not a luxury, it is a necessity. Ours was a law-abiding town largely because the men who tended bar in Haileybury's four hotels were handpicked. They were selected not only for their gravely friendly demeanor, their sagacity, their profound knowledge of prizefighting and current standings in baseball and hockey leagues, but for their diplomatic gifts. They could settle arguments so amiably and maintain such benevolent neutrality in the interests of peace on earth and goodwill to men that belligerents who evinced thirst for each other's blood usually left the bar staggering arm in arm and proclaiming eternal friendship. After all, a hostelry known for mayhem could easily become a hostelry without a license.

There were fights, of course, and even a couple of regrettable killings, but the fights usually ended in the alley with the winner standing drinks all round and no hard feelings. As for the killings, usually accidental, no one really approved. Everyone knew this sort of thing was bound to happen from time to time when high-spirited chaps get a skinful and small grievances are blown up beyond proportion.

The citizens could point to their town with pride. Granted that we owned up to four very wet hotels, on the other side of the ledger we had four Protestant churches, a Roman Catholic cathedral with a palace for the bishop, and a tiny assembly hall where the devout had fits every Friday night. The scales were weighted in favor of the godly.

We also had a real theater and a hockey rink side by side under the same roof. No one ever believed this until they saw it for themselves. Itinerant road companies whispering *Lady Audley's Secret* always wound up hoarse trying to compete with the shrieks of the hockey fans on the other side of the building. A Simon Legree could get mighty confused if the home town scored a goal just as he was doing his worst to Uncle Tom with the blacksnake whip. He wasn't accustomed to a mighty roar of cheers at this point in the drama.

All around us real drama flourished. Out in the wilderness huge bushfires raged in summer and autumn, and snuffed out the lives of prospectors and settlers. Blizzards raged in winter and trapped prospecting parties on the frozen lakes. Penniless men risked their lives in rapids, toiled in the swamps and woods, found gold and became millionaires. Over in the Cobalt camp, bootleggers and high-graders fought running battles with the cops.

All around us, romantic figures strode the plank sidewalks. Big Jack Munro, the "Nevada Kid," was a familiar figure as he shouldered his way through the crowds in the Maple Leaf Hotel. There was Benny Hollinger, who had conned his uncle, the bar-keep at the Matabanick, out of a fifty-dollar grubstake, bought some beans and bacon and went up into the Porcupine country where he staked a block of claims that were to yield gold for the next fifty years.

And then there was another tattered bar-fly with a shaggy beard, known to his indigent intimates as Sandy McIntyre, who latched onto some rocky acreage nearby and lived to see a fabulous gold mine named after him. The McIntyre Mine is still listed on the New York Stock Exchange, but the founder's name wasn't McIntyre at all. Back in England a certain Mrs. Oliphant often wondered where the hell her errant husband had gone, certain of only one thing—that he was bumming his quota of Scotch every day wherever he was. Sandy often speculated on what his life partner's emotions would be if she ever tracked him down and soon found that he was practically swimming in money, which didn't last long because prospectors made only thousands while promoters made millions. But then, it isn't everyone who makes the history books with his name on a big mine even if it is under an alias.

Sandy's fame was eventually challenged by another local character, also from overseas, who set up shop as a guide in Indian country. At that time his wife knew him as Archie Belaney. Archie surfaced in spectacular fashion as Grey Owl, a full-blooded Indian with literary gifts. Not only did he find a publisher for his works on natural history but he went back to England in buckskin garments with a feather in his plaited hair and made it big as a lecturer. Bigwigs who wouldn't have given Archie Belaney the time of day crowded to hear Grey Owl's inside dope on life in the wigwams and the training of beaver as pets. They sought his autograph on the books they bought in gratifying numbers and entertained him at public functions, wrote him up in the papers and told him he was a credit to his race. Privately they were astounded to learn that a genuine, sure-enough redskin could write his own name, much less a book. The bitter howls of "fraud" that went up when Grey Owl was eventually exposed after he went to the Happy Hunting Grounds were not really justified because Archie was a damn good writer and knew his stuff. To this day, school children read his books to learn about beaver and Indian life, and happily revere Grey Owl as one of the best.

A host of other characters made it big, too, in more or less dubious ways. A man from Maine, named Harry Oakes, a dour fellow down to his last buck, boarded the train to Swastika in the dead of winter, went into the Kirkland Lake bush and staked the Lake Shore mine, which was to make him a multi-millionaire and a victim of unsolved murder in Nassau. Ed Hargreaves, our butcher, grubstaked his brother-in-law, a quiet little fellow named Bill Wright, who had staked his own claim next to the Oakes claims, and came up with a mine that made him Canada's wealthiest man. Young Gil LaBine blew in to town from an Ottawa Valley village, became hipped on the subject of pitchblende, which nobody had ever heard of, eventually found his way to Great Bear Lake and discovered the radium that was to help make the first atom bomb.

And our own mayor, Charles Cobbold Farr, was an authentic Remarkable Man. An Englishman of good family, he once worked with the survey party that established the boundary between the provinces of Ontario and Quebec. Then he became a Hudson's Bay Company factor and achieved local distinction as the first white man to run the dangerous Long Sault Rapids in a canoe. He survived to remark that it was a damn sight quicker than walking the portage. Mr. Farr's hurry was explained by the fact that he was on his way to his wedding at the time. The bride's comments were not recorded but she probably said he was a caution.

At the turn of the century, after founding Haileybury on the hillside, Farr induced friends and relatives to emigrate from

England and take up land. Then he talked the government into building a railway into his bailiwick, which consisted largely of rock and scrub bush and where the climate was bitterly described by settlers as ten months of winter followed by two months of rather poor sleighing weather.

Canada, however, is a country so rich in surprises that you can almost always count on the unexpected, the improbable or the impossible. Just when rival politicians were righteously condemning the government for waste of public money on the most useless railway ever built in a country which had already established spectacular records for money-losing trackage, the railway workers hit an utterly unforeseen jackpot outside Haileybury. Their dynamite, which had left a trail of shattered rock for a hundred miles, blew the lid off the fabulous silver bonanza which triggered the Silver Stampede.

The most hilarious episode of Farr's life, however, was when he decided that the newly arrived immigrants were badly treated and sought to prove his point by going to Toronto and disguising himself as a shabby Old Countryman just off the boat. Unfortunately he chose to effect the change of garments in a dark lane beside the King Edward Hotel. He was surprised by a cop who jumped to the conclusion that instead of exchanging respectable attire for the raiment of a bum, he was a bum climbing into clothing purloined from a hotel guest. The researcher was promptly tossed into the pokey.

There Farr decided it would be best to make a frank confession, revealed himself as the mayor of Haileybury and cited the Premier of the province and a dozen other bigwigs as references. The police then concluded that he was not only a bum but a mental case. It was a week before the Chief of Police informed the Premier, as a sidesplitting joke, that some bum who was being held in jail kept insisting that he was on terms of close personal friendship with most of Toronto's bluebloods and that he was even the mayor of Haileybury. The Premier, appalled, realized that this was no joke and Farr was promptly set free with no end of official apologies from all concerned.

As editor of the Haileybury paper, Farr published his

first-hand account of the adventure as an exclusive scoop that ran to many columns and insisted that he had proved his point. It could have happened to any penniless immigrant, he said, no matter how respectable his connections.

The Remarkable Man was always stirring up something. One of his favorite pastimes was to make periodic voyages out onto Lake Temiskaming in his motor boat, the *Jinnie M.* On these excursions he was always accompanied by a couple of bottles and an Irish setter named O'Dog. Eventually he would run out of gasoline and whiskey in that order, an alarm would be sounded, and rescuers would set out with restoratives. Occasionally a second rescue party would be required to embark in search of Rescue Party Number One, by then having a jolly time on board the becalmed *Jinnie M.*

O'Dog always enjoyed these adventures. Actually, he didn't have a name—Farr didn't believe in it. Let other people bestow such cognomens as Towser and Rover on their canine pets. When Farr felt that he required the animal's presence, he merely opened his office door and bawled "Oh, dog!" After a while everyone in town assumed that this was the dog's name and that it was probably of Irish origin.

Another canine character of great fame, a gentle but incredibly ugly bulldog named Cobalt, owned a lawyer whom he visited only on occasion because he was a sort of traveling dog with a passion for riding on trolleys and trains. He spent a good deal of time on the streetcars that ran between Haileybury and Cobalt, presumably on a lifetime pass. A couple of times a year, when he felt the need of a vacation, he would board the southbound train and journey to Toronto, where he would find his way to the aforementioned King Edward Hotel, favored hostelry of all northerners. There he would be welcomed by friends, because everyone in the mining country knew him. After visiting for a few days he would waddle back to Union Station and board the northbound. Unlike the prospectors who did the same thing, he always returned looking refreshed and none the worse for wear.

This, then, was frontier life of a kind that has vanished. It stands to reason we revelled in it. But we didn't. As kids, we were blind to its color. We found it dull because it was the life around us.

No doubt the youngsters in Tombstone and Virginia City complained about their lot too.

"Aw, mom, when are we going to get out of this dumb town."

"What's wrong with it?"

"Everything. Nothing ever happens in Tombstone."

"What do you mean nothing ever happens? How about that big shoot-out at the O.K. Corral last week?"

"That was *last* week. And anyway I missed it. Had to go to school. Besides, what's another shoot-out? Why can't we go back to Philadelphia? We had *fun* there."

There was school, of course. Because our father was the principal, our little comrades had a notion that my brothers and I would be specially favored and that we would get high marks no matter how dumb we were. It didn't work that way. Dad leaned over backward to prove that he didn't believe in nepotism. At the same time he indicated that he expected better than normal performance so that we would be a credit to him. In this I was a disappointment to him.

He was a kind father, a good man, diligent and conscientious who read a chapter from the Bible to us at breakfast and went to church twice every Sunday. On these occasions, during the period of prayer he must have asked the Almighty to give him a hand. And when Divine help failed to materialize he must have asked God just where he had gone wrong, where he had erred, what exactly had he done to deserve me.

The reason for this despair was that he couldn't teach me anything about arithmetic. He often said he was tempted to give up the teaching profession and go into life insurance, because he couldn't even teach his own son to multiply six times twelve. He was clearly in the wrong field and a failure by any reasonable standard.

Somehow I got into high school where I achieved a record

that was remarkable in its way. In three successive years, at examination time, I scored zero in algebra and geometry. I escaped an examination in the fourth year by turning patriot and taking advantage of a wartime dispensation of the Department of Education that gave a student automatic promotion if he would work on a farm from May through August to help boost the nation's agricultural production. My brother Frank and I promptly headed for our grandmother's farm in the Ottawa Valley and enjoyed ourselves enormously because there were two resident uncles to do the work. Our contribution to the Canadian food supply was on the same level as my achievements in mathematics. I tried to learn how to milk a cow once but the animal had a nervous breakdown. Our uncles decided that perhaps we would be more helpful weeding onions. The onion crop that year declined dramatically.

In other years there were other summer jobs because the moment the Spring term ended a boy was supposed to get out from underfoot and prepare himself for life by earning an honest living. One time I worked as a tallyman in a lumber mill. This meant sitting on a bench from seven o'clock every morning, with a one-hour break for lunch, until six in the evening recording the dimensions of the spruce and pine boards that slid by in endless succession as they came from the saws. On my very first day my tally-sheet astonished the office clerk because I managed to triple the normal board-footage of the sawmill.

Another summer I was cook's helper in a road camp in the bush. This meant crawling out of a bunk at four-thirty while stars were still in the sky, setting out the tin plates and cutlery with bowls of prunes and porridge and huge jugs of milk and coffee, serving four meals a day to a fifty-man crew of dour and silent roadbuilders. In my spare time I washed dishes. I ate well but that was about all one could say for that job.

After that I stayed at home and became assistant projectionist at a local movie theater. A glorious job because I could see all the films for free and smooch with the blonde cashier in the dark back row when the boss took over in the booth. The movies were silent, of course, with two projection machines turned by crank. The job held interesting risks—incineration if the nitrate film ever caught fire, a punch on the nose if the cashier's boyfriend happened by.

Another time I became a junior clerk in a bank. This had its social aspect because every morning you called on the downtown merchants who groaned when you handed them drafts for collection. Bank regulations also demanded that *someone* sleep on a cot on the premises at night, with a real automatic under his pillow in case of thieves, who never turned up. I had my turn. A brand-new teller had not, somehow, been informed of this arrangement. When he returned late one night to catch up on a little work he discovered that he had mislaid his door key. So he made entry by the back window.

Awakened by the commotion, I concluded that the thieves had finally got around to their visit. I could see someone climbing in the window so I clutched the automatic in both hands, aimed in the general direction of the marauder and pulled the trigger. It was a good thing I had forgotten to release the safety catch because I was still trying to figure out what had gone wrong when my colleague emerged without a puncture. I probably would have missed him anyway. When he turned on the light and took in the situation he turned pale green and had to sit down for a while, mumbling little prayers of gratitude to Almighty God.

The next day the management decided to leave the bank unmanned and let the thieves take their own chances.

Then, too, during the school year there was a small extracurricular job that had its own peculiar fascination. Like thousands of lads all over North America I became a representative of the Curtis Publishing Company of Philadelphia. In lowlier terms this meant that every Thursday afternoon I peddled *The Saturday Evening Post*. The Curtis people insisted, however, that there was a great difference between peddling and salesmanship. They were glad to sell the magazine, of course, but they were primarily interested in promoting the education of the youth of the land. They sent their young representatives a book which began with an article on Salesmanship As an Art, followed by a chapter on the Importance of the Salesman to the Nation. These were followed by detailed instructions on How to Approach a Prospective Customer, How to Interest Him in the Product and How to Close the Sale. The point was that it just wouldn't do to go around bawling "Saturday Evening Post" on the street corners. That had nothing to do with the art of salesmanship. They also supplied a large canvas sack, plainly labelled "Saturday Evening Post" and a supply of magazines every Thursday.

I found a few regular customers, mostly neighbors, but the hotel lobbies constituted the Big Territory. If I found a traveling man resting from his day's labors and reading the *Cobalt Daily Nugget*, he would soon be interrupted by a small voice piping: "Excuse me, sir, but are you interested in reading?"

Usually he would lower his paper, size up his visitor and say: "Huh?" Deftly I would produce a copy of the *Post* from my sack, move over to his side and go into my pitch. "Sir, for five cents, exactly the cost of your newspaper, you can have hours of reading in the best magazine in the world. In the first place, you get entertainment. This week's *Saturday Evening Post* has a very funny story by Octavus Roy Cohen. There is also a new instalment of a thrilling serial by Louis Joseph Vance. But you get more than mere entertainment. You get education. This issue features an article by Samuel Blythe and another article on The Future of the Automobile. . . ." And so on until the bemused victim fished out his nickel, I gave him his copy and looked around for someone else to annoy.

These exercises in Salesmanship would net me about twenty cents a week and a built-in resistance to anyone who ever tries to sell me anything, because I know his little tricks.

The *Post* was a once-a-week thing, which left a good deal of open time after school and on Saturdays. This vacuum was soon filled. I discovered the composing room of our local weekly, the *Haileyburian*.

Every community had its own newspaper. Some even had

two, for Grit and Tory readers respectively. Unimportant stuff, of no earthly interest to anyone except everyone in town. Certainly of no interest to anyone in the great world outside except the few hundred former natives scattered across the continent who got the paper by mail and commented that there must be a lot of new people moving into the old town because they didn't recognize many of the names any more.

They're gone now, most of them, washed away by the tides of time — the small-town weeklies with their flatbed presses, their banks of type, their dusty offices where editors scrawled the chronicles of vanished times, the composing room walls papered with dusty posters and handbills advertising auction sales and picnics and concerts and horse races, ball games and hockey games. And somewhere out back the bound volumes of back numbers dating all the way to the week the paper was born, pages all yellow now and crumbling to the touch.

Gone now. But when one mourns the passing of the small-town paper one merely laments lost youth, an unrewarding exercise in a world where good things new replace good things old. Maybe its columns were full of trivia. Maybe the newswriting would fail to meet the standards of contemporary journalism. Maybe the editorials abounded in clichés. Who cared and what did it matter? I think it matters when a community loses its local paper because when it does, it loses part of its soul, a part that no one-lung radio station or no resident correspondent for the big city daily a hundred miles away can ever retrieve.

I haunted the *Haileyburian* premises. Maybe it was because of the smell. Every place of employment has its own odor of sanctity. At the sawmill you sniffed fresh pine boards and the wet bark of trees. In the road camp cook-house you smelled stews and beans and pies and bread right out of the oven. The movie theater had its own special fragrance of celluloid and collodion and the blonde cashier's *eau de lilac*. But the composing room of the *Haileyburian* was rich with the smell of Ink!

I became quite a nuisance around there in my off-hours

until the kindly editor, Tom Leishman, effected a deal. He offered to pay me one cent an item for "locals." I thought it was because he recognized journalistic promise, but on subsequent reflection I imagine he merely wanted to get me out of the back shop and into the streets annoying the citizenry instead of himself. Whatever his reason, it worked. Practically every train arrival found me on the station platform bugging travelers to find out where they had been and where they were going. Even the hotel registers yielded a gratifying crop of "Mr. J. Smith and wife from North Bay are visitors in town this week at the Maple Leaf" until Tom Leishman plugged that source.

I got one big story, though. There was a fire in a village three miles out of town. I attended this conflagration personally, almost got run over by the fire truck, was drenched by the fire hose (accidentally, I hoped) and got cussed out by the fire chief because I insisted on interviewing him, notebook at the ready, while he was coping with more immediate problems. I rewrote the story on the office typewriter about a dozen times to give it a distinguished literary flavor. It was a fine story and, with minor alterations, got printed. It was followed the next week by another story about the same fire. This was written by Ye Ed himself and it was apologetic in tone. I had gone and burned down the wrong house.

CHAPTER 9:

Career in Journalism

When I got out of high school in 1919, it was time to make a living. I was given a paper indicating that I had passed but the marks in algebra and geometry were deplorable. Let us say I left by a process of elimination, like a tapeworm.

Haileybury didn't offer much promise. The sawmill had closed down. The movie theater had installed motor-drive. The Gowganda Road reached Gowganda. The bank manager informed me there were minimal opportunities in the banking business for one who always got a different result every time he totted up a column of figures. The *Haileyburian* didn't need a staff reporter and couldn't afford one anyway.

But Cobalt had a daily newspaper, called the *Nugget*. Mining-camp papers always seemed to go in for gaudy and imaginative titles, as witness the immortal *Tombstone Epitaph*. I decided to give it a try. So one morning my mother ironed a fresh shirt for me, inspected my shoes, straightened my tie, told me the world was full of disappointments which must be met with good cheer, and gave me a kiss. I thought I was merely going on a journey of five miles, but she knew how long that journey was going to be.

I took the trolley to Cobalt and sought an interview with Mr. Browning, editor of the *Nugget*. He was a gentle man, soft of voice, kind of manner, who said yes, they could use a young reporter who was not afraid of hard work and who was willing to learn. I could begin immediately, at nine dollars a week.

My career was under way.

It began with a crash course in journalism conducted by Dan Cushing, the news editor. It took about three minutes and consisted of one lecture.

"The most important thing is to get the names right," said Mr. Cushing. "Nobody likes to see his name spelled wrong. Remember that."

"Spell the names right."

"Also get the addresses right," continued my mentor. "Last year some bum was thrown into the pokey for being drunk and disorderly and he gave his address as 22 Fourth Avenue. See anything wrong with that?"

"No, sir."

"He didn't live there," said Cushing. "The Baptist minister lived there."

"Oh."

"That reporter should have checked. That reporter is now working underground at the O'Brien Mine, a job I wouldn't wish on a dog. Understand?"

"Yes, sir. Check the addresses and get them right."

Mr. Cushing seized his black pencil and attacked some copy on his desk. I was about to withdraw from his presence when he swung his chair around.

"One more thing."

"Yes, sir."

"Don't use the word *very* in a sentence."

"Very."

"I hate it. That's all."

I departed, thinking that there had to be more to newspaper work.

A few years earlier Cobalt would have been a fine place for any young fellow who sought excitement in newspaper work, but this was 1919, and I was in the wrong town. Like one of her own aging madams with a little money in the bank and a lusty past to contemplate, the Cobalt mining camp had settled down and become respectable. No longer did crowds swarm around the railway station. Some of the oldtimers still hung around, but they were a nostalgic lot who spent their time trading lies about the good old days. The action had shifted to the gold camps farther north. Silver mining, Cobalt's claim to fame, was just an industry now with about as much excitement and adventure as the gravel business.

Cobalt did have a YMCA. This told the whole story — in four letters. You could pick up news at the YMCA. Basketball scores, for example. And organizations devoted to the public good were always holding meetings in its dismal rooms. You could pick up little news items by phoning the clergy. They were generous with baptisms, stray weddings of no social importance, the latest doings of the Epworth League or the Ladies' Aid, plans for the annual Sunday School picnic or the Christmas concert. Stirring stuff. You could also pick up stories of a gloomier sort at the furniture store, where coffins were somehow classed as furniture, with embalming out back as a sideline. No one at that time had thought to give the establishment a bit of class and genteel domestic atmosphere by calling it a parlor or a home. News of higher dramatic content emanated from the fire hall, police court, magistrate's court and the town office but these claims were already staked out by staff reporter Frank Lendrum. All mining news belonged to Jim McRae, who eventually became a millionaire because he learned how to read mining company reports and sift fact from fiction.

This didn't leave very much for the rookie. I didn't mind because I didn't plan to stay in newspaperdom a minute longer than it took to break into the big magazines as an author. In otherwise idle time I took to tapping out little poems and stories destined for Mencken's *Smart Set*, which always sent them back. I was composing one of these one day after the paper had gone to press when Dan Cushing looked in.

"What are you writing?"

"I'm trying to write a short story."

"What's it about?"

This was embarrassing.

"It's — um — it's about a fellow and his sister."

"Well, what happens?"

"It hasn't got much of a plot. I figure on sending it to *Smart Set*. They don't go in much for plot, like most other magazines."

"If it's a story at all, it's got to have a plot. What do they do, this fellow and his sister?"

"They meet each other. Kinda by accident."

"You mean they never met up before?"

"Oh, sure. But the sister — you see — she's gone wrong. And this young fellow, he doesn't know much about girls and he's curious, see?"

"You got a brand-new angle there, son," said Cushing. "Then what happens?"

"Well, like I said, they meet up with each other by accident. Sort of a coincidence."

"Already this story is loaded with suspense. Will you get on with it, for God's sake? Where do they meet?"

I gulped.

"In a whorehouse."

Cushing stared at me. "Did you say in a whorehouse?"

"Yes, sir."

"Another brand-new angle. But, by God, you're original. I've got to say that for you." He mused. "In a whorehouse. I'll be goddammed."

"It's a kind of modern story," I explained. "Like Sherwood Anderson. Not like O. Henry."

"Damn right it isn't." Cushing stared at me again. "You ever been in a whorehouse?"

"Not yet."

"Nor ever," he shouted, pointing a finger at me. "You hear me? Man's tool makes more trouble for him than anything else he's got." Cushing shook his head thoughtfully. "Anyhow, they won't buy your story."

"What makes you so sure?"

"Because you've never been in a whorehouse. It won't be convincing." He looked at me and sighed. "So you're one of those, huh? I was afraid of it."

"One of those what?"

"One of those reporters who want to be writers. I've met dozens of them. They wind up being lousy writers *and* lousy reporters too. Every one of them with a punk first chapter of a punk novel in the bottom drawer of his desk. Never a second chapter, mind. Just the first. Or the first act of a punk play. Just the first act. Or even poetry, by God. At least that's what they call it. Dreadful stuff. Never rhymes."

I began to wonder if Dan Cushing had been snooping through my desk. Maybe he had found some of my poetry. But it rhymed, most of the time, anyway.

"It's better to be a damn good newspaperman than a lousy writer. Any day. Know why? Because there aren't many damn good newspapermen and there are thousands of lousy writers, that's why."

"Richard Harding Davis. . . ."

"Don't," exploded Cushing, "don't throw Richard Harding Davis at me. That show-off ruined more promising reporters than booze ever did. In the first place he was a punk novelist. In the second place he wasn't even a good newspaperman." Mr. Cushing was breathing a little heavily by this time. He pointed the finger at me again. "You want to know why reporters who want to be writers wind up nowhere?"

"Why?"

"Because they're in the wrong business."

"But a reporter meets all kinds of people and finds all kinds of real-life material and learns how to write quickly, so when he gets to writing books. . . ."

"Crap!" said Mr. Cushing.

I couldn't think of a devastating reply to that and I wouldn't have dared make it if I had.

"First of all, there is no place for fine writing in a good news story. In the lead you put the who, the what, the where, the when and if necessary the how and that's all. No fancy work. Try sneaking in any fine writing, any embroidery and I'll cut it because it isn't good newswriting. The readers don't want it and I don't like it, so that's that."

"Yes, sir."

"Want to know why this is the wrong business for a fellow who wants to be a writer?"

"I'd appreciate it."

"Partly because a newspaperman writes stories that are full of facts. A writer doesn't. He makes them up. The two don't go together."

"But. . . ."

"Don't argue with me. I *know*. But the big reason is that there isn't enough time."

"After hours?"

"After what hours? You've had it easy around here so far, whacking out little pieces about what goes on at the YMCA. An honest-to-God newspaperman is a newspaperman twenty-four hours a day. He works like a dog. If he has any spare time he should be out screwing or drinking or hunting or fishing or what have you, maybe even spending a few hours with his family. One thing sure, he shouldn't be farting around with words. And that," concluded Dan Cushing, "is why you're in the wrong business if you have notions about being a writer."

He got up.

"I've got to go to a meeting," he said. "A fellow tipped me off. Committee has to figure out how to raise enough money to keep the Y going for another year."

At the door he looked back.

"That is what is really going on at the YMCA," he said and departed.

I pondered Dan Cushing's good advice for all of thirty seconds. Then, like most people who accept advice only when it confirms what they have already decided to do anyway, I dismissed it from my mind on the ground that it really didn't apply to me. I went back to my siblings who met up in the whorehouse, which was a damn sight more interesting than anything that ever happened in the YMCA. I finished the story and sent it off. Mr. Cushing was correct in his prediction; they didn't accept it. But the rejection slip carried a personal comment from the great Mencken. It read: *Naive. HLM.*

My lack of stature came to be useful to Dan Cushing.

(When you stop growing at five feet three you have problems. It is all very well to console oneself with the thought that Napoleon was a very short man, but Napoleon had a horse.) Cushing sent me to cover a meeting of the miners' union, whose members had a mighty distrust of the *Nugget* and had a standing order that no representative of the paper should be admitted to its conclaves. Because I didn't look like a reporter I got in somehow, but made the mistake of producing my little notebook to jot down an account of the meeting. This was stupid, because I was immediately escorted out by a couple of gentle, but very large, miners.

Undaunted, however, Cushing assigned me to another event where my lack of stature might get me by.

The Prince of Wales (later the King of England for a while) made a tour of Canada, Cobalt included. The Prince announced a desire to see the inside of a silver mine and the O'Brien was nominated. Dan Cushing assigned me to this event. He was smiling strangely when he informed me of the honor. I realized why when I reached the mine and learned that the *Nugget* was barred from the underground regions.

However, after the Prince had vanished beneath the surface, I found a waterproof three sizes too big for me and boarded the next cage right behind a portly correspondent of the august *London Times*. He was a large man who looked as if he wore two waterproofs. I snuggled close to him. In a tunnel, the Prince was listening with profound attention as the mine manager, Angus Campbell, explained the mysteries of silver mining. I fished out my notebook and surfaced under the royal nose to jot down any comments he might make.

This was a mistake. Mr. Campbell stared in disbelief and summoned an aide to escort me to the next cage going back up.

A few years ago, even at the age of eighty-three, Mr. Campbell still remembered this incident. I think it bothered him. I could have been a Bolshevik with a bomb in that waterproof pocket.

Mr. Cushing was pleased, although he didn't believe it until the O'Brien management called up to protest my enterprise. Chuckling, he apologized and promised it wouldn't happen again. He slashed away at my story with his black pencil and cut out all my adjectives, but it made the front page that afternoon.

I took home five extra copies of the *Nugget* that night.

My mother mailed a copy to her sister in Brandon, Manitoba, and placed a clipping of the story in the family Bible. My father sent a copy to his mother in the Ottawa Valley.

I presented a copy to my girl who told me I was a genius and she didn't know how anybody could think up all those words. I said it was easy. Just took a little training. It was how Dickens got his start. She said if Dickens could do it, I could do it, too, probably even better, and how old was Dickens when he got married?

After a few months of learning how to spell names correctly and street addresses exactly, I discovered through the "Male Help Wanted" column of the Toronto *Globe* that experienced reporters were in demand all over Ontario. Any week you could take your pick of a dozen openings. On the principle that I had nothing whatever to lose, I answered all the ads. Consequently, to my great astonishment, I found myself engaged by the *Sudbury Star* at the glittering salary of twenty-five dollars a week.

Dan Cushing of the *Nugget* received this news with deflating calmness.

My mother cried. My father presented me with one of the new safety razors and refrained from good advice. He had done all he could; the rest was up to Providence.

My three brothers concealed their grief bravely. My brother, Frank, who would now have a whole bed to himself, insisted on helping me pack and carried my suitcase to the railway station a good half hour before the southbound train was due.

A dozen former classmates assembled on the platform with an impromptu brass band to make sure I wouldn't change my mind. They even borrowed a drum from the Salvation Army. The band created such an ungodly racket that, when I climbed on board, fellow travelers wanted to know what the hell the celebration was all about.

My hometown on the hillside overlooking the great blue expanse of Lake Temiskaming disappeared. The jackpine, poplars and gray rocks of northern wilderness flashed past the train windows. Fame and fortune lay ahead.

CHAPTER 10:

Mr. Mason, "the Boss Around Here"

Then, in 1920, Sudbury was a rowdy, brawling railway center and mining town in the middle of a region that produced more nickel than any other place in the world. Although the community itself rejoiced in lawns, flower gardens and even a beautiful lake, the surrounding countryside was a forbidding jungle of barren rock that resembled a Wellsian vision of the mountains of the moon. There was a reason for this.

Five miles to the west of the town the International Nickel Company mined nickel and copper ore for the enrichment of Americans. Five miles to the east the Mond Nickel Company did the same for the enrichment of Englishmen. The ore, once mined, was roasted in open beds and sulfur was a primary ingredient of this process. Every night a devastating fog descended upon the outlying area, somehow sparing Sudbury from its worst effects. Occasionally townspeople who found themselves abroad at three o'clock in the morning when the wind was right blundered through this fog; grumbling a little, they comforted themselves with the thought that it didn't happen every night and evolved theories that the sulfur was somehow good for the lungs, which it wasn't. Air pollution hadn't been invented then, but if it had they would have bragged that the nickel district was its original Canadian home.

Sudbury was and is to this day a tough place, a no-nonsense town, and work on the *Sudbury Star*, I quickly discovered, was no different. I reported to Bill Mason, who was a large, blustery man with the truculent appearance of a surly bulldog. "When you work for the *Sudbury Star*," he said, leaning back in his swivel chair with his thumbs in his waistcoat pockets, "you begin with the understanding that we are entitled to your services twenty-four hours a day. If you don't like the idea you can quit right now."

I didn't care much for the idea but I had come a long way, two hundred miles, and it seemed a little foolish to resign before I began. Nor did it seem propitious to quote from a memorable performance of *Uncle Tom's Cabin* by the touring Tom Marks players in the Plaza Theatre back home. *"Massa, you may own dis ole black body but mah soul belong to God!"* It was always greeted with resounding cheers, brought down the house in fact, but I didn't think Mason would appreciate it.

"I am the boss around here. Let's get that straight." He gazed at me sourly. Somehow I got the impression that he despised reporters. "You will report for work every morning at eight o'clock. Not eight-thirty or eight-fifteen or even eight-five. Eight sharp. On the dot."

"I'm always very punctual," I told him.

"You goddamn better be," he told me. "When you come in you will edit the country correspondence and scalp the city dailies for time copy to keep the machines going. At ten o'clock you will cover police court which sometimes goes on for hours. And any sonofabitch tries to bribe you to keep his name out of the paper, tell him to go to hell. Just you try to pick up a few bucks that way and I'll not only find out, but I'll kick your ass all the way back to Haileybury. After police court," he continued, "you write your copy and then you cover the town hall, the undertakers, the mining recorder's office, the police station and the fire hall. Not by phone. Personally."

I began to see myself scooting around town on roller skates.

"Also the provincial police office and the railway stations. And the hotels, of course. Interview any important visitors and find out what they're up to. In between times drop into the stores and talk to people. Never know what you'll dig up."

I was about to ask him what I would have to do in my spare time, but he beat me to it.

"In the evenings you'll cover meetings. There's always some kind of meeting. School board, town council — sometimes those councilors chew the fat until two in the morning. But if you leave before they adjourn they're liable to slip something over."

"Oh yes," he said by way of afterthought. "Sports, of course. Ball games. Hockey in winter."

A few days later he remembered to instruct me that it was also a reporter's duty to rewrite and file major news stories for the Canadian Press wire under the terms of the franchise, and subsequently he allowed me to write the lesser editorials and an allegedly humorous column, preferably local in flavor. I adapted most of it from the resident geniuses of the *Chicago Tribune* and *New York Herald*, on the principle that if you have to steal from somebody there is no point in fooling around with second-raters.

This was my introduction to W.E. Mason, then a rising publishing tycoon and later the owner of two newspapers, two radio stations, two theaters, a bus line, a couple of apartment buildings and a million dollars. He was a giant who had started humbly by setting up shop as a job printer in Sudbury. He went on, as most job printers did, to turn out a newspaper. That the town already had a couple of newspapers mattered not at all to the aggressive Mason who regarded opposition as something to be bulldozed into extinction.

By the time I arrived he was well on his way. One opposition paper had been demolished, the other was tottering and the *Star* was appearing twice a week. Every Wednesday and Saturday afternoon he turned a swarm of yelping newsboys loose on the town. Everyone who bought the paper got full value for his nickel. Circulation rose.

Whenever circulation went up a little Bill Mason adjusted his advertising rates a little, too. Upward. When he demolished the last stronghold of the opposition — a sad little weekly called the *Mining News* — he adjusted rates so enthusiastically that the advertisers moaned pitifully. Bill Mason ignored their anguish. "If you don't like it," he advised them cheerfully, "go advertise somewhere else." This was unanswerable and he knew it. So did the advertisers. There wasn't another paper within a hundred miles.

A few stubborn merchants refused to go along. Eventually, one by one, these hold-outs returned to the fold only to discover that their recalcitrance was punishable by a further twist of the screw. After a while further boosts were accepted submissively and viewed as natural calamities of business life in Sudbury, like creek floods in Spring and frozen water pipes in Winter.

And God help any advertiser who got a little behind in his account. Almost any day visitors to the public office of the *Star* could hear Mason bellowing over the phone at some delinquent, loudly identified by name. "What the hell do you mean, times are tough?" he would shout. "I'm running a paper, not a charity. You owe me forty-seven dollars and by God I want that dough by five o'clock or I'll sue you."

There was nothing subtle about the Mason collection techniques.

Toward members of his staff, who depended on the *Star* for their livelihood, he was equally ruthless. Tramp printers, who usually slunk into town with a bad case of the shakes and a spare shirt in need of laundering, were frequently victims of his wrath. Let such a slave pi a stick of type, hoping no one would notice until he repaired the damage, and Mason would materialize instantly before the offender like the Angel of Destruction in a medieval play. "Why you butterfingered slob, what the hell is going on out here?" he would bellow in a voice audible all the way out to the railway crossing on Elm Street. "Great Jumping Jesus H. Christ, can't you even set a simple stick of type? You call yourself a printer? Get outa my shop. Go get your time. You're fired!" Because it wasn't a union shop, all the other printers (with the exception of the foreman, who was indispensable and knew it) would tremble in their shoes and put on a feverish show of activity as Mason dematerialized.

Later, around the bar of the Nickel Range Hotel, members of the composing room staff would comfort the victim and console him over farewell beers. After a few more beers they would make their own plans for escape. These plans were always contingent on saving enough money to pay their debts and get out of town; always they involved moving on to some mythical printers' paradise where the boss was a human being and one got paid double-time for over-time. Invariably, too, these plans involved well-rehearsed speeches of denunciation to Mason's face or punching him in the nose. But none of these things ever happened. Nobody could afford it.

If it is complimentary to observe that Bill Mason pursued power and wealth with awesome ruthlessness, then I raise my hat to him. He may have confronted problems far beyond the ken of any young reporter. Perhaps he had to be ruthless to survive at all. My feelings toward him were ambivalent. I admired him in a fascinated sort of way. As a boss I thought he was a holy terror.

Since a reporter traveled on foot—even Mason didn't own a car—I went flying around town like a small comet in orbit, from office to police court to town hall, to railway station to hotels, to provincial police office to fire hall to town police station and back to the office again, then out to fires, car crashes, ball games, school board meetings, town council sessions and the annual picnic of the Presbyterian Church Sunday School.

There was no scarcity of news. Police court was usually good for a couple of columns a day, most of the offenses originating in the great swindle known as prohibition. Toward this assault on human liberty the solid citizens of Sudbury adopted an understanding attitude: they didn't believe in it, so they ignored it. A local brewery flourished all through the era, beer was generally available in the hotels and there was a four-block area where you could knock on any door and find strong drink at slightly inflated prices. This region was called Geezler Town but nobody ever knew why. To the police it was invisible and therefore did not exist.

To show that their hearts were in the right place, the police resorted to a process known as "keeping the streets clean." Basically, this meant that they chivvied the poor and friendless. Sudbury was full of mine workers — Finns, Ukranians, Russians, Italians, Poles and French-Canadians—who lived in crowded boarding houses where they had little to do but drink and gamble. If one of them wandered outside, he was fair game for a cop. Whenever crime slacked off, a flying raid on a boarding house always reaped a dozen bewildered wretches bound to be guilty of something. And every Spring hundreds of happy lumberjacks converged on the community after a winter of back-breaking toil. Any lumberjack worth his salt just naturally got roaring drunk when he hit town. The cops netted them in carload lots. Casual visitors to Sudbury often commented favorably on its orderly aspect; never a bum or a drunk in sight. Clearly, they felt, it was a respectable, God-fearing, law-abiding town.

Breaches of the Temperance Act did not produce all the stories, however. Plenty of gaudier tales unfolded in police court. The Finns, for example, carried knives and used them to settle their differences, which were usually political because there were Red Finns and White Finns. A melancholy group, they were sometimes given to blowing themselves up with dynamite, an effective but messy way of solving personal problems. The Italians fought over the division of bootlegging territories and regarded a gun as the most satisfactory weapon because it was so unanswerable in argument. The French-Canadians, who disputed over money or women in that order, belabored one another with any weapon that came to hand, be it a whiffletree, a beer bottle or another French-Canadian. Anglo-Saxons, prone to fight over anything that occurred to them at the moment, used their fists. A punch on the nose vindicated one's honor and was not so likely to land one in jail. The Chinese, a humble, hardworking bunch, were always being arrested in droves for whiling away their lonely hours gambling among themselves. As for the Indians, they kept out of trouble simply by keeping out of town. They knew better. A white man can be a mighty friendly fellow on a fishing trip,

Little Beaver, but don't let it fool you. Stay in the bush if you want to stay out of jail.

In one bad year I covered three murder trials. The first case on the docket provoked a good deal of soul-searching. The defendant was a small, frightened, undernourished eleven-year-old who looked about eight. One of a large family who lived in a dismal bushland shack, he was charged with killing one of his numerous brothers with a bullet from a twenty-two rifle he used for shooting rabbits. He declared over and over that he thought the gun was empty and quaked with terror in the prisoner's dock because he faced death on the gallows. The jury, however, was merciful. The twelve good men returned a verdict of manslaughter. This was a great relief to citizens who were having profoundly bothersome second thoughts about a system that could send a child to the scaffold in District Jail courtyard. It was a narrow squeak. Everyone was happy, of course, that the youngster would spend a few years in reformatory, where he would be educated and improved by association with a lot of other bad kids who had been brushed under the rug.

The second trial proved, if it needed proving, that the collective mind of a jury works in remarkable ways. A mine worker had quit his job, cashed a hefty paycheck and disappeared. He had no family and a handful of acquaintances assumed that he had moved on to another mining camp. A few weeks later his body was found in the bush outside town. His head had been blown off by a shotgun.

Pat O'Connell, a detective with an unfortunate cast in one eye, didn't have much to work on, but he picked up the trail of a fellow workman who had also quit at about the same time as the victim, tracked him all the way to a remote village in Quebec and brought him back in handcuffs.

At the trial O'Connell not only linked the prisoner with a shotgun, but produced the dead man's paycheck stub which he said he found in the defendant's possession. An admiring public regarded O'Connell as a sleuth of uncommon ability, right up there with Sherlock Holmes.

To general astonishment, however, the jury brought in a verdict of acquittal. This astonishment was apparently shared by the man from Quebec but he recovered rapidly and vanished from the courtroom in about ten seconds, as if afraid the jury might have second thoughts and decide to hang him after all.

Later I asked one of the jurymen why they had brought down that verdict in such an open-and-shut case.

"Reasonable doubt," he said. "The detective could have planted that paycheck stub on the guy. We didn't trust him."

"Why not?"

"He couldn't look us in the eye."

"How could he? He had a cast."

"Oh? Just the same, he had a pretty shifty look. Wouldn't trust a man like that any farther that I could throw a bull by the tail."

The third case was a reporter's dream. It involved violence, illicit sex and a triangle, which gave me a wonderful opportunity to turn out columns of heart-wrenching prose for three whole days. It happened, predictably enough, in a railway town. Because railwaymen were away from home a lot on predictable schedules of departure and return, all railway towns were popularly regarded as hotbeds of adultery, smoky forerunners of Peyton Place with freight and passenger service. One of these sizzling communities yielded up a passionate matron accused of doing in her lover with a bullet from a thirty-eight.

No one in town could believe it because the lady was no less a personage than the secretary of the International Association of Engineers' Wives. In this office she had once gone all the way to Denver to attend a convention, expenses paid. This alone was enough to convince the populace that the cops had made a grievous error. Ladies of such prominence don't have lovers and if they do, they certainly don't go around ventilating them with a thirty-eight.

Evidence at the inquest, however, indicated that even a high officer of the IAEW could be susceptible to human frailty.

Apparently happily married, the woman became extremely unhappy when she suspected that her next-door neighbor, a burly widower, was enjoying a little supplementary romance, with whom, she didn't know. But she meant to find out, so she kept a jealous eye on his house.

One evening while her husband was out on his run, she invited the lonely widower over for supper. When he arrived dressed in his Sunday best, her worst suspicions were confirmed. Obviously he was up to something because it wasn't Sunday. When she wanted to know why he was wearing his good suit and a white shirt on a weekday, he gave the lame excuse that he was expecting a visit from his uncle. This was such a patent falsehood that she pursued her inquiries. Relentlessly grilled, he broke down and admitted that he was all dressed up to meet a fur buyer that evening at the YMCA.

The widower may have been a redoubtable lover but he was a deplorable liar.

When he returned home his neighbor mounted watch by her kitchen window, saw him leave by his front door — no doubt trying to look like a man on his way to the YMCA—and then saw him circle around and sneak in again by a side door. Then she saw a female figure enter by the front door. A little later, when she saw the house lights go out, she armed herself with a revolver and went visiting by the back door.

As a consequence, the engineer was killed and the lady was booked into the local calaboose at her own request. She showed a lamentable lack of contrition and, in fact, told the police that she was was quite happy about the whole thing. It gave her a feeling of peace, she said. She also said that when she invaded the engineer's bedroom—out of sheer curiosity— she rousted out the pretty wife of a railway accountant and that the agitated guest fled without even exchanging condolences.

The trial drew packed houses. Excitement reached a crescendo when the defendant herself took the stand. She admitted everything but said she didn't do it on purpose.

Members of the jury, already convinced by experience that women are notoriously poor shots under the best conditions, took a practical view of the matter. A Crown Attorney who asked them to believe that a woman could hit any kind of target with a thirty-eight, especially in the dark, was simply flying in the face of common sense. The lady was forthwith acquitted, to uproarious applause which subsided only when the judge threatened to clear the courtroom.

"And now may I go back to my husband?" she asked.

The judge said, kindly, that she could.

The big reconciliation scene, unfortunately, fell a little flat. It lacked the tears, the sobs, the embraces that would seem to be appropriate at such a moment. Maybe her husband was just shy; he shook hands with her.

I never did get around to using any of this lively material in fiction. Some writers have a blind spot when it comes to material in which they have been involved, even on the periphery. The lady with the gun eventually yielded a radio play in a series I worked up about Canadian crimes, but that was documentary stuff, requiring no invention. There was no mystery about it— how can you have a mystery when the chief suspect confesses right off the bat?

CHAPTER 11:

The Northland

When I became a reporter, I had no intention of making newspaper journalism a career, no secret hope of some day becoming an editor or publisher. Instead, I wanted to become an author.

In Canada in the Twenties such an ambition, if I had dared say it aloud, would have been regarded as imbecilic. Authors, unless they were also clergymen or professors, just didn't make any money and even then they didn't make much. This answered everything.

Thanks to my Irish ancestry, however, I was bull-headed and stubborn about the matter. Newspaper work, especially on the *Sudbury Star*, left practically no time for after-hours ventures into literature. But by staying awake until two o'clock one morning, I did manage to write a short story, supposedly humorous. I sent it to the *Toronto Star Weekly*, the magazine section of a large newspaper which came out with the Saturday edition. The *Weekly* printed quite a bit of serious writing, usually by reporters who worked on the *Daily*. One of them was a bright young fellow called Ernest Hemingway and there was another by the name of Callaghan. The paper once sent Hemingway up to Sudbury on a wild-goose story about a man who said he had discovered a huge coal deposit right beside a nickel mine.

I told Hemingway, just another Toronto reporter, that the

whole thing was a fraud, so he went back to the city and salvaged the trip by doing a piece about Sudbury. It was a good piece, too, but he innocently mentioned seeing a lot of girls on the streets. This was quite true; the local kids didn't have anything else to do but walk up and down. Indignant citizens, however, got the idea that he implied that their daughters were training for whorehood and wrote letters to the papers about it for days afterward. This is not what he had in mind. He just didn't know Sudbury.

The editor of the *Star Weekly*, J.C. Cranston, was a kind man with a soft spot in his heart for Canadian writers, especially the younger ones. He knew they had to begin by getting their work into print. He published my story with an illustration by Jim Frise, the staff cartoonist of enormous talent. Not only did Cranston print it, he paid me ten dollars and asked for more.

I have no doubt a Nobel Prize winner feels pretty good when he learns that he has made it, but he can't feel any more elated than a novice writer who sees his story in print. For several days I made my rounds in a happy state of bemused idiocy, imagining that everyone in town was saying: "Look, look! There's the chap who had a story in the *Star Weekly*. With his name on it. Remarkable piece of work. Some day we'll be proud to say we knew him." But nobody mentioned it. Proximity to genius has that effect on people. It makes them shy.

For several weeks I stayed in the office until two o'clock every morning, writing more little stories for Mr. Cranston. And damned if he didn't buy them all. I decided it was time Mason realized that he had a valuable man on his staff, a man obviously worthy of a raise, so I showed him clippings of my little fictions.

"Where did you write this crap?" he inquired.

"Here in the office. After hours," I added thoughtfully.

"On my typewriter," he snorted. "With my ribbons. On my paper. Using my postage stamps too, I'll bet. And after hours be damned. On my time."

I decided, before it occurred to Mason to charge me rent,

that the request for a little boost in the paycheck might better be deferred. A fine sense of timing warned me that this was definitely not the moment.

"The *Star Weekly* must be goddamn hard up for stuff to fill their lousy paper. Oh well, from now on you won't have any spare time for turning out this junk. Hockey season starts next week."

What he meant was that Sudbury was about to surrender to a state of complete lunacy for the next four months. The job of recording even the minor aspects of this bizarre period would call for superhuman energies. And he was right.

I was qualified to cope with it, after a fashion. As a kid in Haileybury I had seen professional hockey and found it interesting because it had a gratifying quality of the unexpected: the star who won a game for his club one night was apt to turn up in a rival uniform at the next encounter. This had no end of effect on the betting odds (much as if Johnny Bench showed up in a Montreal Expos' uniform, with no advance warning, for a game against the Cincinnati Reds).

If the professional games were good, the amateur hockey provided by the Sudbury Wolves and their bitter rivals, the Sault Ste. Marie Greyhounds, was merely fabulous. Even today the surviving fans, now toothless and rheumy-eyed, fondly recall it as the most exciting stuff they've ever seen. Amateurism merely meant then, as it does now, that the players weren't supposed to admit that they were paid. They were good enough, in fact, to qualify for any professional club and, in time, most of them did when the money was right. The Wolves became the first edition of the New York Americans and the Greyhounds provided backbone for the New York Rangers and the Montreal Maroons. Many of them are in the Hockey Hall of Fame today.

It is futile, of course, to draw any comparisons between hockey in the Twenties and hockey in the Seventies. The game differs vastly, although the basics haven't changed and a great player then would be a great one today. Stick-handling, all but a lost art these days, was highly esteemed because a forward pass was not permissible. To see Shorty Green or Bill Cook thread their way through a barricade of swinging sticks, to see Charlie Langlois or Babe Donnelly wind up behind the net and go zigzagging all the way down the ice to draw out the goalie and slam the puck into the net was to see hockey at its thrilling best.

With only two substitutes the regulars had to be iron men to go at top speed for sixty minutes. No such nonsense as a minute of ice time and a three-minute rest so that a man would be fresh and eager to play another game the next night. In this league the next game was next week, so players went all out for three periods of battle and collapsed in a state of exhaustion when it was over.

A goalkeeper had to stay on his feet. Today's goalies, who spend a lot of time making like seals at lunch, would be appalled by this ruling; nevertheless shutouts were not uncommon. And, because the games were played on natural ice, the teams would play in slush or on a watery surface during a January thaw or an early Spring, which merely added to the unpredictability of the outcome.

As for officials at the games in Sudbury, there was just a referee, usually a sports writer from Toronto. The regulars included little Bill Tackaberry of the *Mail and Empire*, pugnacious Mike Rodden of the *Globe* and the great Lou Marsh of the *Star*. They signaled halts in play by ringing a hand bell which often came in handy if some howling fan leaned too far over the rail to offer criticism. An unwise comment implying that the referee would be better off armed with a tin cup and a few pencils or that his mother had won awards at the Canadian National Exhibition dog show could earn a sharp rap over the head with the bell. Mike Rodden was especially deft with his elbows. Leaning backward over the rail he could bloody a critic's nose without losing track of the play for an instant. Afterward, if the home team lost, the referee sometimes had to battle his way out of the dressing room through a hostile delegation. Then his most effective weapons were his skates, which he donned like gloves and came out swinging. Sudbury assignments called for danger pay. A referee with guts enough to come back for another game would have qualified for a Victoria Cross if this guerdon had been awarded in peacetime.

Each club appointed a goal umpire, who was therefore — and rightly—suspected of bias. He had to stand out on the ice behind the net and wave a handkerchief to signal a goal, which meant that he seldom dared blow his nose, no matter how distressed. It was a risky job. He could easily find himself the main ingredient of a human sandwich when a couple of reckless opponents, going hell-for-leather, collided behind the goal. If he allowed or disallowed a debatable goal, it behooved him to keep a sharp lookout for the next player who came steaming in behind the net, all stick and elbows and bent on running over him by accident. These perils tended to keep goal umpires honest.

But the real aura of excitement was created by the fans. From November to March Sudbury gave itself up to mass lunacy. This was proven by the fact that on the night before a game scores of fans would huddle in line outside the rink to await the opening of the box office next morning. Baseball and football fans have been known to do this, but on a winter night in Sudbury the thermometer frequently descended to twenty degrees or more below zero. The doughty fans would build small bonfires to warm themselves. Anyone who would endure these hardships to see a hockey game had to be some kind of a nut.

Fans, however, were not content with just watching the games; they insisted on living them over again in every detail on the sports page. No mere one-column survey of the highlights would do — they demanded, and got, a play-by-play account to the extent of about half a page. And when a game was played out of town, those who couldn't make the two hundred-mile trip by train demanded instant information. This was provided by the Canadian Pacific Railway's telegraph people, who stole a page from World Series baseball and heavyweight championship coverage by offering play-by-play wire service. To offer this service they needed someone who would show up at the rink and dictate a running account of the play to an operator with a fast finger on the key.

By this time, the duties of sports editor had been added to my other tasks at the *Sudbury Star*. Although I was already a hockey fan, I knew as little about inside hockey as I did about the higher calculus, a fact which soon became apparent to everybody. I was a dreadful hockey writer. Enthusiastic, yes. But awful.

As I was the only one around, the telegraph people invited me to dictate the play-by-play accounts to their man. When a game was played in Sudbury I would take up position beside the operator, start talking, and the keys would start clicking. Two hundred and fifty miles away, in Sault Ste. Marie, a man at a typewriter would translate the clicks into words and hammer out pages of script, in duplicate. These pages would be rushed to the local movie theaters, the lounges of the curling clubs and the hockey clubs, to all places where the Sault Ste. Marie fans could gather.

There they would be read aloud, to the cheers or groans of the assembled listeners. As soon as one batch of copy came to an end, another batch would arrive from the telegraph office. This would go on, at intervals, for the duration of the game. Admittedly, it was a little confusing in the movie houses because the film in progress would be resumed during the intervals and cut short when the manager would bound on stage to read aloud the details of another five minutes of action in the distant rink. ·

When a game was played in Sault Ste. Marie the procedure was reversed. I accompanied the Wolves to Sault Ste. Marie as sports editor for the *Sudbury Star*, and at the beginning of a game I would amble up to my perch beside the operator and do my stuff again.

So even before radio arrived I became one of hockey's first broadcasters with the power to interrupt pool games, curling matches or the screen adventures of Colleen Moore and Richard Dix while hundreds of fans hung on my words and read from the long takes of copy. As it turned out, I was, in effect, paving the way for my son Brian who has established his own fame as a hockey commentator on television. His audiences take instant communication for granted; mine didn't. They always thought it was mighty ingenious.

When I told Bill Mason that I was being rewarded at the rate of five dollars per game, he affected downright incredulity. He commented on the color, accuracy and wit of my reports. He said he practically rolled in the aisles at the Princess Theatre. The whole town, he declared, relished each performance and waited impatiently for the next. I was being exploited, he said, pointing out that the telegraph people were getting twenty-five dollars from each club and movie theater in town for the service and piling up tremendous profits at my expense. Clearly, I didn't realize my own worth. Where else could they find anyone with such a gift for instant phrasing, such an infinite knowledge of hockey on the fly?

I agreed that he had a point.

Out of his concern for my welfare, Bill Mason then advised me to go to the telegraph people immediately and demand twenty dollars a game. "Stand up for your rights." he said. "Don't let them get away with that five dollar stuff. They can't do without you."

Feeling extremely confident, I went to Dan Bowen at the CPR telegraph office and told him I thought my services were worth twenty dollars a game.

"You must be crazy," said Bowen. "We can't pay that."

"Fifteen?" I suggested hopefully.

"Out of the question."

"I would be willing," I said, "to come down to ten."

"Double what you're getting now. Impossible."

I surrendered and said I guessed I could go on doing it for five.

"I wouldn't think of it," said Bowen. "You wouldn't be happy. And it is not our policy to employ anyone who isn't completely happy. Let's forget the whole deal."

I walked out of there, no longer the only hockey broadcaster in that region, and not very clear in my mind how it had come about. Subsequent accounts were done by the telegraph operator working solo. Apparently no one noticed the difference. The CPR saved five dollars and Bill Mason slapped me on the back and said he was proud of me for standing up for my rights.

This is how one young man learned an important fact of life; no one is indispensable.

Bill Mason, seeking new worlds, bought the paper on which I had served my apprenticeship, the *Nugget*, and moved it out of the fading silver camp of Cobalt, lock, stock and staff, a hundred miles south to the railway town of North Bay. There he set out to joyfully demolish three rival weeklies.

They had been in North Bay for a long time, moping along, running the local news, printing the local ads, their job presses turning out auction sale bills and fliers for grocery stores with an occasional big job on the program for the annual Fall Fair. For the publishers, who were also editors, reporters and pressmen, life was pleasantly uneventful. They knew they would never be rich but there was enough work for all, not a threatening cloud in the sky, and they basked in peace. Then, like villagers under Vesuvius, they were jolted into panic and consternation when Mason erupted into their lives.

He set up residence for a while, established the *Nugget* as a big paper with a wire service and newsboys turned loose like a pack of hounds yelping in the streets. He established cut rates on job printing orders, he bludgeoned advertisers into submission. He introduced appalled employees of the crumbling opposition to the Mason way of life.

The *Nugget* covered all the North Bay news and more. Mason hired correspondents in all the one-paper towns east, west and north, all the way up the Temiskaming and Northern Ontario Railway for more than two hundred miles.

Within a few months of his takeover a big story broke.

It broke, of all places, in my home town. Haileybury. And I had to cover it — a story that struck at the roots of my life.

Northern Ontario is a hard country. Winter is long and

bitter. It descends inexorably in October and does not relinquish its grip until the ice of its ten thousand lakes has melted seven months later. It is a harsh and hostile land.

One can cope with zero weather. But the summers brought menace of another kind — bushfires raging out of control, gobbling up the wilderness timber.

In Haileybury we knew about bushfires. I was a youngster in 1911 when one of these fires swept the Porcupine camp, levelled it to the ground and took scores of lives. This was a raw, new mining camp of three little towns — Golden City, Pottsville and South Porcupine — where four rich gold mines had drawn sourdoughs and miners from all over the world. The railway had just come in. On a hot day in July, when the temperature was 100 in the shade, dozens of small fires in the bush and muskeg joined together in a hot wind that created its own awesome draft. It swept down on the camp on a twenty-mile front with burning treetops flying through the air.

That was the day the Nevada Kid took over with a gun in his hand and set up a bucket brigade. (The kid was Jack Munro, a Cape Breton prizefighter who once clobbered the great Jim Jeffries in a four-round exhibition and was clobbered in return when it counted for the heavyweight title.) That was when a freight carload of dynamite blew up and overturned all the boats and canoes in the lake when their passengers thought they were on the way to safety. That was when Little Eva, mine captain at the West Dome, took his wife and youngster and sixteen mine workers down the shaft as a refuge and they all perished. Little Eva was Bob Weiss, who weighed over 300 pounds and used to play football in the States. There is still a place on Porcupine Lake they call Deadman's Point where seventeen victims were buried in rough boxes after the fire. They never did make an exact account of the dead, but the total came to a hundred.

Then there was the big Matheson fire of the summer of 1916, different because it was a settlers' fire. It swept half a dozen towns and half a million acres of farmland, killing 200 people. From Haileybury, miles away, I could see the whole northern sky glowing like a furnace. That was when a priest at a little village called Nushka led his people into a railway cut with steep clay banks and they all died. That was when a settler took four families, twenty-two people in all, into his root-house and none came out alive. I remembered the railway station the next evening, the platform stacked with rough boxes and coffins. I remembered the relief train coming down from the north jammed with men, women and children, their faces blackened and clothing burned, on their way to our hospital. Most had their eyes bandaged and some were blinded for life. They groped their way out of coaches that were scorched black.

In Haileybury, people had learned to live with the menace. Every year there were scattered fires in the bush west of the town. Every year there were days when the foul mist of smoke from distant fires hung over the hillside and the lake. But every year, as more and more settlers cleared their land, the danger seemed to recede.

On the fourth of October, 1922, after a long dry spell, the usual fires were burning in the region but these were isolated blazes where settlers had been burning slash in their clearings. Then a high wind came up, a wind that became an Autumn gale. The small fires merged and became a conflagration that roared across eighteen townships, 2,000 square miles of countryside. It hit Haileybury and a dozen other communities like a red hot cyclone, with less than an hour of warning.

From the *Nugget* office news editor Ed Loney headed north by train. Then the wires went down. In Sudbury all we knew was that a final flash from Cobalt said Haileybury had been destroyed. That night Mason ordered me to North Bay by taxi, a wild eighty-mile drive over a gravel road. Railway headquarters was the only source of news and that news was sketchy, confusing and all bad. I managed to patch together enough of it to fill a front page of the *Nugget* and by mid-morning we put out an extra.

And I was grateful to be busy. There was little but rumor in the air and as usual the rumors were black; a rumor always begins with the worst assumptions and expands from there. I thought of my father and mother, my brothers and our home as phones jangled, typewriters and linotypes clattered. I even resorted to silent prayer, although I was badly out of practice and had a dismal feeling that it was a little late anyway. Whatever had happened, for good or ill, belonged to the previous afternoon and was already settled one way or the other.

Then the word came through: a relief train from the north country was entering the North Bay railway yards. I headed for the station. As the train came to a stop and weary people emerged from the coaches, I caught a glimpse of my mother, then my small brother. When my mother saw me, her familiar bright smile turned me inside out. We hugged and kissed each other.

"How about Dad? Frank? Dick?"

"They're safe. I saw them in Cobalt this morning. They'll be down on the next train."

She told me how the fire had swept the town, how my father had dismissed his school and instructed the older pupils to take the younger children home, how he had found room for her and my younger brother in one of the few cars that raced back and forth between Haileybury and Cobalt that wild afternoon. Then he remained with his other sons to face the danger.

The platform was becoming crowded with old friends and neighbors so I became a newspaperman again and talked to them, picked up fragments of their stories, got my mother and brother to a hotel and talked the clerk into giving them a room. Then we sat down and I fished a wad of copy paper from my pocket.

"Now then, Mom — let's start at the beginning."

She was always a calm woman and she told the story clearly. I left them and went back to the office to write up my eyewitness account. My father and my other brothers arrived on the next train and told me the rest: the scenes of confusion and terror when three-quarters of the town went up in flames within two hours, how they took refuge with hundreds of others in the icy lake and watched Haileybury become a vast glowing ember on the hillside as a snowstorm swept in.

Two days later I went up to Haileybury to do a follow-up story. The hillside was a smoky ruin under falling snow. Every familiar landmark had been erased so completely that at first I couldn't even find the street where we had lived. At last I discovered the place where our home had been—a black hole in the ground with a charred bathtub perched on a heap of rubble. Across the road were the ruins of Paul Cobbold's home which had always looked as if it had been miraculously transported, rose garden and all, from some old English village. Paul Cobbold had been the local weatherman. Every morning, for years, I had watched him emerge from a doorway like some quaint figure in a mechanical clock, to read his instruments and jot down the figures in his little notebook. My mother said she had last seen him there in the smoke and wind when the fire was beginning to ravage the town. Paul and his frail little wife were victims of the fire. Next door another Englishman, the gloomy, taciturn Mr. Elphik, whom no one knew very well, was a charred skeleton in the garden of the home he had refused to leave.

Twelve died in Haileybury, thirty more in the small villages and farmlands to the north. It was ironic that the only part of Haileybury left untouched was "Millionaire's Row" where the mining executives and wealthier people lived in their fine homes in the north end. For a while people revived that old English pub song which deplores the contrasting lots of rich and poor and ends, *"Isn't it a blooming shyme."*

A good town, like a good man, is not easily destroyed. The people came back. My father returned and built another house on the site of the old. A new school was constructed, a new court house rose on the hill, new churches, new stores, new banks, new homes soon appeared. Within two years the community was on its feet and today it is again the loveliest town in the Northland. But although the local people cheerfully insist, in the words of the *Cobalt Song*, that "It's the best old town I know," to me it was never the same again. The landmarks of childhood were gone.

CHAPTER 12:

Never Tell the Truth About an Amateur Show

Back in Sudbury, I returned to whizzing about the streets, whacking out half a million words of copy a year and enjoying my work, too stupid to realize that better conditions prevailed on practically every other newspaper on earth.

Among my dozens of other assignments, I also enjoyed the role of dramatic critic. Sudbury was one of the towns on the Trans-Canada Theaters' circuit which aimed to provide audiences with British theatrical fare. A company would depart from London, cross the sea by ship to Halifax and then cross Canada in a series of breathtaking 500-mile jumps. A week in Sudbury helped pay travel costs between Ottawa and Fort William.

For a while we lived high in terms of entertainment. Martin Harvey, in *The Only Way*, Cyril Maude, in *Grumpy*, H.V. Esmond, in *Eliza Comes to Stay*, walked the stage of the Grand Opera House and I talked with all of them. The interview was always the same. The visiting star found Canadian distances a little more than startling, but enjoyed the opportunity of bringing good British theater to a colony of such infinite vigor and promise.

The only one who said anything new was a British music-hall comedian named Harry Tait, a beefy, red-faced fellow who portrayed a fumbling Britisher in a series of comedy sketches. Tait, like many comedians, was very funny on stage and very matter-of-fact the moment he got out of costume and makeup. One night over an after-show supper of ham and eggs, he told me of a bitter grievance he entertained toward a blasted American juggler fellow who had played in England and rewarded his hospitality by pinching several of his best acts. One of them was called "Motoring," another "Fishing" and another "Billiards." I had watched the "Billiards" sketch that night and had seen Harry Tait reduce the audience to hysterics by his antics with a billiard cue made of rubber. The name of the chap who had purloined his best bits was W.C. Fields, confided Tait. He was apoplectic about the whole matter because now he was finding on his cross-country tour that some people were anticipating his biggest laughs. On investigation he discovered that they had seen Fields doing the same stuff in vaudeville and on the New York stage and regarded Harry Tait as a talentless imitator. He was moodily devouring his ham and eggs when I expressed condolences and left him.

And inevitably, of course, there was Harry Lauder, who also learned his trade in the music halls. Short, stocky, bandy-legged, whenever he came on stage, chuckling and beaming, his kilts swinging, he captured his audience and didn't let it go for two and a half hours. The show brought in every Scotsman within a thousand miles. They cheered every Scottish song — even wept at some of them — and roared at every mother-in-law joke. It was familiar to many of them because they had heard Lauder in the Old Country, but theirs was the joy of recognition. It didn't matter that the jokes were old and it didn't matter that they had heard the songs before and had listened to them again and again on records. Harry was their man, the personification of Scottish frugality, Scottish humor and Scottish fondness for whiskey. His was the triumph of a theatrical personality; he knew exactly what his audience wanted and he gave it to them in overflowing measure.

Of a different stamp were McIntyre and Heath, blackface comedians from the American stage. Breaking a jump between Winnipeg and Toronto (which is not so much a jump as a giant leap) they scheduled a stopover performance in Sudbury, only their train was late and they didn't arrive until two o'clock in the morning. When McIntyre and Heath learned that the audience was still waiting and that no one had left the theater, they announced that such patience deserved their best.

McIntyre and Heath worked in blackface but they were white men from the world of minstrel shows. Bert Williams was about the only black comedian who could cross the color line to white audiences at that time. They fell in the tradition of Conroy and Lemaire, and later the Two Black Crows and Amos and Andy; the fat, dimwitted, obtuse comic and his foil, a stringy, excitable little fellow who fed him the good lines. We howled at their stuff until five o'clock in the morning and stumbled out of the theater agreeing that it was a night well spent.

I made a half-hearted try for an interview but the stage manager begged off. McIntyre and Heath were too exhausted, and an interview wouldn't work anyway, he said. McIntyre hadn't spoken to Heath and vice versa for about five years except on stage. When I asked the reason for this remarkable state of affairs between a pair who seemed such jovial companions behind the footlights, he said he didn't know. Apparently there had been a quarrel, probably about some matter of little importance, and as a result they simply decided to stop speaking to one another.

When the Grand Theatre threatened to remain dark for a week there was always an amateur show to fill the breach. Like most amateur shows, these were invariably dreadful. Once in a while an impresario would hit town, hunt around for a Worthy Cause and offer to put on a show for a sizable share of the gross receipts. He would present credentials showing that he was a theatrical man of parts, a playwright, a producer, a director and actor. He would dredge up a moth-eaten script which he claimed to have written all by himself. Later, no one doubted this claim. He would assume entire responsibility. All he needed were a few amateur performers whom he would train and rehearse to the point where they would be as talented as any road artists we had ever seen. It always turned out to be just another amateur show.

There came a time, however, when a gent named Theodore H. Bird descended on Sudbury and conned the local Children's Aid Society into sponsoring his *magnum opus*, called *My Dream Girl*, guaranteed to be chockfull of romance, comedy, stirring drama and tuneful songs. For the next two weeks Mr. Bird toiled with his performers. Costumes were made or rented or borrowed. Scenery was built and installed at the Grand.

One big "effect" spectacle gave a little trouble. It called for a storm at sea and Theodore H. Bird should have known better, but he promised it would be completely convincing. It always had been. You solved it by setting up a small, phoney lighthouse constructed of cardboard at the extreme rear of the stage. An electric light bulb was installed in this lighthouse and a stage-hand was instructed to switch it off at intervals.

Then strips of carpet were laid across the stage from wing to wing and more stage-hands were shown how to undulate the carpets to provide the effect of rolling waves. In broad daylight it was singularly unconvincing, but Theodore H. Bird promised that when stage lights were lowered and a small boat-full of performers were hauled across the stage by rope it would deceive any audience on earth. They would smell the salty air of the sea and duck to escape the spray.

It didn't turn out to be quite that convincing. Apart from the fact that the script was lamentable, the songs and music imitative of sources not worthy of imitating and the performances as haltingly stilted as could be expected, *My Dream Girl* ran into complete disaster when the great Storm at Sea blew up. When Theodore H. Bird gave his stage-hands their instructions he forgot one little detail: he neglected to remind someone to scrub and sweep the stage. During the weeks of diligent rehearsals, his performers had tracked in a good deal of mud which had turned to dust. When the stage-hands in the wings got their cue to undulate the strips of carpet, they fell to with a zest they had never shown before; they whipped those carpets up and down with joyous vigor. As the boat was hauled through the storm and the one-bulb lighthouse blinked in the background, a great cloud of dust rose from the ocean, drifted out over the footlights and engulfed the audience. It was the sort of fine, dry old dust that gets into the throat and makes one cough, that creeps into the nose and makes one sneeze. In no time at all the entire audience of *My Dream Girl* set up such a storm of barking, strangling, snorting and sneezing that they drowned out the plaintive "Ahoys" from the performers in the boat.

The dust didn't settle for a long while. Most members of the audience were there only because they were related to an amateur perfomer. They saw no reason to court asphyxiation as a family duty and they headed toward the exit door. Some irreverent souls actually thought the catastrophe was funny and made their departure with streaming eyes. The audience was dwindling rapidly as *My Dream Girl* limped toward the final curtain. Backstage, the male performers were cursing and female performers were weeping.

After witnessing this disaster I decided that it was worthy of a front-page account. Not only that, I thought it was time to discourage amateur theatrical performances in which performers and local Good Causes were the willing victims of con men who played on their vanity.

Ridicule would have been superfluous. All I did was sit down at the typewriter and tap out a straightforward account of what happened. Perhaps I did mention that it seemed a little odd that the squire of the manor insisted on wearing riding breeches and a bowler hat in the ballroom scene but I did not yield to a temptation to be funny about the Storm at Sea. I merely described it in considerable detail. As for the local performers, I stated that they were all so gifted it was a pity Theodore H. Bird had not provided them with material commensurate with their obvious talents. Nothing more than that.

But I did shatter an unwritten law of newswriting in small communities, which is that one must never tell the truth about an amateur show. It simply isn't done. Perhaps there is a tradition of sportsmanship about it, like refraining from shooting birds on the ground. Perhaps it is based on more practical reasons; the leading lady may be related to a merchant who spends money on advertising.

Bill Mason was away on a business trip at the time, otherwise his sound business instinct would have taken over and he would have killed the piece the moment he set eyes on it. It ran on the front page the next afternoon and after an hour or so the phones began to ring and all hell broke loose.

When Mason got back the town was in turmoil. Those who wouldn't be caught dead at an amateur show were laughing themselves sick and the more they laughed the more furious became those who had been involved. Subscribers were phoning to cancel their subscriptions, advertisers were phoning to cancel advertising, the Children's Aid was demanding apologies, other organizations were holding meetings to pass motions of censure.

The leading man advanced his vacation by two months and disappeared. The leading lady wasn't seen in public for days. Theodore H. Bird vanished. An officer of the Children's Aid caught up to me in the bar of the Nickel Range and had to be restrained from punching me on the nose.

Bill Mason called me into his office and gave me a tongue-lashing that outdid any of his previous performances in that line. How, he wanted to know, could I have been so stupid? Didn't I know that amateur shows were sacred? Did I have any idea what this monumental goof had cost the *Star* in subscriptions and advertising revenue, in prestige and goodwill?

Beyond remarking that subscribers always came back, I took it in humble silence. Then I noticed that Mason seemed to be running down, unable to sustain his high level of outrage and indignation. His voice faltered for a second and a strange look came over his face. He chuckled. The chuckle turned to a snicker, the snicker an outright laugh and finally he roared, wiping the tears from his eyes.

"Oh, Lord, Mac! That was a funny story," he gasped. "That cloud of dust from the sea—the squire in his riding boots at the ball—oh, I'm sorry I wasn't there." He pounded the desk and laughed as I had never known him to laugh before.

The guy was human after all.

In spite of my boners, and because of Mason's ruthless attitude toward news gathering, the *Star*'s circulation grew — so much so that we acquired a girl reporter, fresh out of high school, who attended to weddings and other events that passed for society in the town. For a while her presence gave me a livelier interest in the day's work. A blonde of challenging virtue, she kept me in a state of frustrated concupiscence which was clearly very bad for my health. When I pointed this out to her she displayed a deplorable lack of concern — I was given to understand that if she had been interested in health care she would have taken up nursing.

In any case I abandoned the siege and went back to writing poetry — it was less troublesome. Like most poetry written by callow young men it was pretty somber stuff and usually began with the premise that some day we would all be in the cemetery, which naturally led to the conclusion, in more or less impeccable rhyme, that we should live it up a little while we were spared. The girls always expressed admiration for the poems and the poet, but they always seemed to desert me for some uncouth suitor who owned a car. One day I came across a couple of these poems, under the byline of the lass who inspired them, in a minor magazine. Although I was flattered by this recognition and forgave the young lady when she explained that she had been pressed for funds, I couldn't help feeling that I should have had a credit at the very least. But I did admire her ingenuity. The incident was educative. A man is always learning something new about women, even if he lives to see his hundredth birthday.

Then we acquired Beckett.

A tall gangling man, he showed up from nowhere as tramp reporters and printers always did. But Beckett was no tramp. Obviously born with a copy pencil behind his ear, he took over as managing editor as if the chair had been waiting for him since the paper was founded.

He was a traveled man. Name a newspaper and Beckett had worked on it—not long, perhaps, but he had been there. Name a major city in North America and Beckett knew it well. Name a major news story of the past twenty-five years and Beckett had covered it. Name a public figure of sport, stage, crime or politics and Beckett had not only interviewed him but was privy to some delightful scandal to lend color to the recollection.

He had worked for Walter Howey on the *Chicago Tribune* and survived. He had worked for Hearst and shared the honor, along with a few hundred others, of being fired by the great man on several occasions. He had even found time to explore the seamy bypaths of his profession as publicity man for a circus and press agent for a movie star; he had even done managerial stints for Jack Johnson and Stanley Ketchel, world champions of the prize ring. Of these two he confided that Johnson had indeed taken a dive at Havana and that Ketchel's notoriety as a great lover was well deserved. The fighter, Beckett said, was never content with bedding down with just one girl. He insisted on two so that a second-stringer was always available in case of exhaustion, and it wouldn't be Ketchel's. As for the movie star, my eyebrows flew up when Beckett reminisced about some of that idol's little peculiarities.

I came to the conclusion that although Beckett was probably the most engaging human being I had ever encountered, he also had to be the most prodigious romancer. Then he invited me up to his hotel room one evening for a drink—no furnished lodgings for this man—and he dug clippings out of his trunk. Damned if he hadn't been telling the truth. He *had* worked everywhere. And he *had* met everyone.

From then on we were friends. He was a newspaperman of vast experience who had complete command of his craft. He could write heads without counting on his fingers. He could call up a news source—and within a month he had conjured up dozens of them — ask a few questions on the phone, listen without taking notes, swing around to his typewriter, bang out a story, head it up and despatch it to the composing room in ten minutes flat. All the while he would be chuckling happily and puffing on an enormous pipe so diligently that his desk was wreathed in a permanent cloud.

Only once did I ever see him perturbed. This was on the morning he reached for the large box of kitchen matches he kept close at hand, lit his pipe, blew on the match and tossed it back over his shoulder into the wastebasket. This familiar gesture he employed at least fifty times a day with no untoward result.

Until that morning.

I heard crackling noises and looked around. Beckett was hunched over his desk, editing copy.

"Mr. Beckett."

"Be with you in a minute. I'm busy."

"Your wastebasket is on fire."

Beckett towered to his feet as if he'd been goosed. He stared incredulously at the wastebasket.

"Great Scott!" he said. "So it is."

Then he gave a bellow of laughter and tried to stamp out the blaze by planting his foot in the wastebasket. But it was a wire basket and when he stamped a second time he found his foot was trapped. Still laughing uproariously, Beckett lunged around the office with one leg of his pants on fire, trying to kick himself free. Every kick sent blazing papers in all directions. The society editor screamed and bent over to pick up one of the papers.

If you have never seen a blonde society editor kicked in the ass by a flaming wastebasket, you have missed one of the rare experiences of journalism.

Beckett finally got rid of the wastebasket by booting it so lustily that it flew into my wastebasket and set off another blaze. The blonde fled, spanking frantically at her butt. Half a dozen fires were in progress before someone rushed in from the business office with an extinguisher. The rescuer, with commendable presence of mind, put Beckett out first, then turned to saving the office and probably the entire building from destruction.

Beckett surveyed the damage, chortling. "Editor sets fire to himself. First time it ever happened."

Then he sat down again, refilled his pipe, blew out the match with care, tossed it back over his shoulder into the wastebasket and resumed his work. He chuckled joyously all the rest of the morning and broke into occasional hoots. "Editor sets fire to himself," he repeated every once in a while.

I was relieved that Mason was away at the time and said so. "Too damn bad he wasn't here," snorted Beckett." I've told him a dozen times wire wastebaskets are no use in a news office. Too small. What we need are great big metal wastebaskets like we had on the *San Francisco Examiner*. Soon as Mason comes back I'll tell him."

He did and we got a large metal wastebasket about the size of an oil drum. Beckett was the only man to whom Mason ever listened; he was also the only man, to my knowledge, whom Mason ever respected.

Beckett said the secret was simple. Mason, he agreed, was a bastard but bastards never bothered Beckett because he had met hundreds of them and knew how to handle them. The newspaper business was full of bastards. It was a sort of natural phenomenon like fleas on a dog. Some of the bastards Beckett had encountered, especially on the Hearst papers, were so steeped in bastardy that they made Mason look like some kind of fumbling amateur bastard who tried hard but had never become a full-blown bastard and never would because he lacked the talent for it.

"You simply let them know you won't stand for any god-damn nonsense, you laugh like hell when they ask you to do something stupid and if they keep it up you merely tell them to go screw themselves and you move on to another paper. There are always plenty of bastards but then there are always plenty of papers. And not too many first-rate newspapermen, as they know very well."

Beckett didn't stay long. His departure was not explosive. It was not triggered by any dispute so he didn't even tell Mason to screw himself, which disappointed me considerably because

I had been waiting a long time. Beckett merely said it was time to get moving again—he was becoming a little restless. He put in a few long-distance calls and calmly announced that he had connected as manager editor of the *Montreal Herald*. Once again I thought he was stretching it a little and once again I discovered that he had told the truth.

Before he left we had a talk. "You say you want to be a writer," he said, puffing at his pipe and grinning.

"Do you think I could be?"

"Why not? Writers are good newspapermen who make things up. You have a good vocabulary. You write with punch. And some of those things you did for the *Star Weekly* weren't bad at all."

"I mean a *good* writer."

"Who knows? Depends on what's inside you. Talent. Some have a little and make it stick. Some have a lot and mess it up. The best have a lot of talent and use it right, but even that isn't enough. You need luck, which means timing. Not much point in being recognized as a good one after you're dead, is there?"

"Well—posterity . . . ."

"To hell with posterity," Beckett snapped. "It never paid a writer's rent." He looked me over as if seeing me for the first time. "Trouble is, you haven't lived very much yet. So you make do with what you've got and work like hell."

"I'm not afraid of work. You know that."

"Newspaper work is easy. The material is around you all the time and all you do is set it down. A writer has to drag the stuff out of his head. Alone all day at a desk, dreaming it up, working it out. Good writers work like sonsabitches. And God help their wives."

"But it must be very satisfying."

"Good writers are never satisfied. That's why they're lousy businessmen when it comes to selling their stuff. It never comes out as good as they want so they're apologetic about it and get swindled. As for self-expression, forget that crap. You write for readers, not for yourself."

"But as a Canadian writer...."

"Oh no!" groaned Beckett. "Don't give me that line. Canadians regard a writer as a nut. Until the Americans or the English tell them he's all right they think he is just naturally no damn good. And then they only respect him if he makes a great deal of dough."

"Do you think I could make a living?"

"Writing for American magazines, yes." Beckett took another drag at the pipe. "If you've got anything on the ball they'll smell it out. But you'll never be any kind of a writer unless you give it a good hard try, so quit fooling around. You got a hundred bucks?"

"Just about."

Beckett picked up a copy of that day's paper, turned the pages until he found the classified ads. "Just saw it this afternoon. The very thing for you."

Summer cottage to rent, furnished.
Boat. $100 season.

"Rent it," advised Beckett. "Move in and spend all summer writing stories."

"But I'd have to give up my job."

"Of course," laughed Beckett. "That's the whole idea."

"How will I eat?"

It seemed a reasonable question but Beckett glowered. A trifling issue. In a subsequent decade he would have said, "That's your problem." Now he merely remarked, "You'll have to work that out for yourself."

"I'll think about it."

"Don't wait too long. I've met scores of old newspapermen who wanted to be writers and never got around to it."

He got up to go, then looked back over his shoulder. "If you ever get into a jam or need a job give me a call. Collect. I can always find a spot for you."

A kind man, Beckett, hence a good man.

After he went away I investigated the cottage for rent. A secluded cabin in the bush, it fronted a sandy beach on a bay three miles down Lake Ramsey. It was a small place, sketchily furnished, with two bedrooms on either side of a large kitchen. And a screened veranda. There was no road, no electricity, not even a well. Drinking water came from a spring in the woods.

It was a fine place. Yet when I thought of giving up the security of that weekly paycheck from the *Star* in exchange for the hazards of independent existence, my spirit quailed. I decided I had better think it over a little longer.

The problem, like many problems, solved itself.

A few mornings later Bill Mason arrived at the office in a surly mood. After bawling out a couple of hirelings in the advertising department, he came into the newsroom and sat down to grumble about the way things were going. The whole paper, he said, was going to pot. News coverage was sloppy. Nothing had gone right since Beckett left. The front page lacked zip. A citizen's name had been incorrectly spelled. Big stories were being played down and little stories were being played up. The humor column wasn't funny any more. I had been late for work two mornings in a row. What the hell was the matter with me anyway?

The burden of all this was familiar. I had heard it, with variations, on a hundred other mornings. I could have said that with Beckett's departure I was overworked again but it didn't seem important. This exasperated Bill Mason.

"And the hell of it is," he exploded finally, "I don't think you even give a damn because you're not even *listening* to me."

Perhaps an invisible Beckett tapped me on the shoulder and whispered, "Now is the time." So I put down my copy pencil, got to my feet, reached to the rack for my straw hat and put it on my head.

Then, to my infinite astonishment, I heard myself tell Mason to go fuck himself.

I doubt if life holds any greater satisfaction.

Then I walked out of there, away from it all.

CHAPTER 13:

Literature and the Good Life

Fifty years later I might have grown a beard, forsworn baths, acquired a guitar and a girl with stringy hair and set out on the highway to find myself. I was a good deal more conservative, perhaps less adventurous. I merely bought a second-hand typewriter, rented the cabin for a season and moved in with a stock of provisions and two cases of beer. A green canoe provided transportation between the cabin and Sudbury, three miles up the lake.

Besides, I was very serious about making a living as a writer of fiction. It would be gratifying to report that this came easily, but it didn't. The trouble was that I wanted to begin at the top, in *Harper's Magazine* or the *Atlantic Monthly*. The stories they printed seemed to have very little plot, which was convenient because I wasn't very good at making up plots. Clearly, in these great magazines it wasn't the story that counted but how you told it. Plots were for popular magazine writers, not for talented authors in embryo.

I had my standards and these were the standards of Henry Louis Mencken. They were acquired years before when I was going to high school and discovered the *Smart Set*, a magazine with a cover as misleading as its name, which proved that you should never judge by appearances. One picked it up on the assumption that it was much like *Snappy Stories*, with a content of mildly erotic fiction. But instead, before you knew it, you were reading Scott Fitzgerald's marvelous *Diamond As Big As the Ritz*, or something by Willa Cather, Somerset Maugham, or Theodore Dreiser.

Other wonders of an unexpected and refreshing kind lay in the back of the magazine. Theatrical criticism, for example, by a man named George Jean Nathan, who informed the reader that all the popular Broadway plays he longed to see were boring things written by dunces, and that all the good plays were being written by men he had never heard of — Eugene O'Neil, Ferenc Molnár, Sean O'Casey and George Bernard Shaw.

And then there were the essays of H.L. Mencken himself. A reader learned from Mr. Mencken that although Gene Stratton Porter headed the best-seller lists year after year, this did not necessarily mean that she was a good writer. He also learned that such eminent authors as Harold Bell Wright, Zane Gray and Robert W. Chambers, to say nothing of Reverend Henry Van Dyke, were imbeciles who wrote for the entertainment of morons. Mencken ridiculed these idols with such hilarious contempt that they could never be taken seriously again. On the other hand, he had solid praise for a writer named Joseph Conrad, a Polish sailor who had mastered the English language so thoroughly that he made better use of it than anyone else alive.

Mencken also gave instruction in current affairs. I discovered, to my astonishment, that many famous people, hitherto regarded with reverence because they held high positions and got their names in the papers, were fools, impostors, charlatans or downright idiots. Billy Sunday, prominent man of God, may have been a good baseball player in his time but now he was nothing more than a windy con man admired only by boobs. William Jennings Bryan, who *looked* like a great statesman, was a pious fraud. Even the President of the United States, who in those days was regarded as being beyond criticism, became a ward-heeler, a tool of crooks, a buffoon given to blather which made no sense to anyone at any time. This seemed pretty blasphemous to me and I kept a sharp eye on the news for a month after that, sure that Mencken would be arrested and shot as a traitor. It was one thing to suggest that politicians and college professors were scoundrels, or to ridicule Billy Sunday, an ordained clergyman, but to denounce the head of the American government — after all!

In today's climate, where protest is a religion and no person or institution, past or present, is even remotely sacred, it is difficult to conceive of that time not so long ago when the masses surrendered placidly to mass deceits and shied away from any opinion that conflicted with the common view. Iconoclasm was rare and came as a shock. True, Robert W. Ingersoll had set a disturbing precedent but Ingersoll, obviously, was the Antichrist and dismissed accordingly. An editor named Brann created ructions in the columns of a paper he printed down in Kansas, but Brann was clearly off his rocker, a show-off and a nut. The only comforting thing about this new fellow, Mencken, was that he was of German parentage, which explained everything. If World War I, just concluded, had proven anything at all, it was that all Germans were dedicated to the destruction of all that was sane and decent in the American Way of Life.

But no retribution fell upon Mr. Mencken. He stayed out of jail and went on smashing public idols. Nowadays it is fashionable to decry him as an entertaining but destructive stylist. I read him with joy, learning among other things to enjoy literature. Convinced that he was my own private discovery, I was unaware that all over North America young people were also discovering him and crowding through the door that he opened for them — the door to a world where everything was upside down, where nothing was what it appeared to be and where one learned that popular opinions were wrong nine times out of ten.

Mencken's magazine, now known as the *American Mercury*, became my monthly Bible. Mencken thought so highly of Conrad that I read *Outcast of the Islands* and was enchanted by the style. Now when I wrote a gloomy little tale for the *Atlantic Monthly*, I began using two pages to get a character into a room and another two pages explaining why he was there. My stories became not only long-winded but lugubrious, deep stuff, with five-syllable words, five-line sentences and paragraphs that went on for pages about dismal people in dismal conditions. Then the *Mercury* introduced me to Sherwood Anderson, who wrote very brief stories about small-town people and wasn't overly concerned with plot.

Output increased, but these stories returned as rapidly as the others. Even so, it never occurred to me that I might be in the wrong business. Every writer, I knew, suffered discouragement and rejection—look at Zane Gray. Here was a humble dentist who believed in himself and wrote six books, all of them rejected, before he was recognized. So I went on writing dreadful stories under the illusion that it was only a matter of time.

I began to look into some magazines that might not be as picky as the *Atlantic Monthly*. An article in the *American Mercury*, written by a man who churned out a million words a year for the pulps, explained how simple it was to find publication —to say nothing of large sums of money—in this fertile field. The secret, he confided, was to treat the whole business with the contempt it deserved, to realize that all one's readers were morons and to understand that all editors were cynics outvying each other to print the most dreadful rubbish they could find.

I read a few of these magazines and decided that the anonymous scrivener may have been unduly harsh. One yarn, by a practitioner named A.E. Apple, lauded on the cover as an ornament to his art, told how a master criminal named Rafferty looted the entire city of New York in twenty-four hours. Rafferty began by inventing an invisible, tasteless, odorless gas which instantly paralysed everyone who inhaled it and left them frozen in whatever activity they were engaged in at the time. Later, when they came to, they would carry on as usual, not realizing that anything untoward had happened.

In the meantime, however, all the banks and stores would be left open to the depredations of Rafferty. Obviously he was going to need a little help, a problem he solved by importing a thousand Bolsheviks who were naturally grateful to escape from Russia and get a stake in the Land of Opportunity. His solution to the problem of getting his helpers past Ellis Island was equally ingenious. Rafferty merely chartered a vessel, loaded his Bolsheviks into barrels and smuggled them through customs disguised as pickles. Then he pried open the pickle barrels, paralysed the city and turned his imported Bolsheviks loose with large sacks to accommodate the plunder.

I later discovered that Mr. A. E. Apple was a fellow Canadian, although such is our national indifference to genius that Mr. Apple's name appears in no lists of acceptable Canadian literati. Surely any writer who could dream up a scheme to smuggle a thousand Bolsheviks disguised as pickles is deserving of some recognition by his countrymen. After reading Mr. Apple's tale I thought that such fiction lay beyond my talents. It is merely sensible to recognize one's limitations, I cautioned myself.

Eventually, however, I blundered into it. Every night, at Coniston and Copper Cliff, cupola cars full of molten slag from the smelters would be hauled out along precipitous hillsides and dumped. This apocalyptic spectacle could be seen for miles; the orange glow lit up the countryside and was reflected in the sky. It occurred to me that any unsuspecting wanderer who got lost in that region at night would be in for a shocking surprise along about pouring time. Perhaps there was a story idea in this.

The victim, of course, would have to be deserving of such a fate, so I worked out a fiction about a scamp who was making a clean getaway from pursuing lawmen when he mistook the slag dump for a railway embankment and the slag train for a way freight, thereby meeting a fiery come-uppance for his sins. This grisly tale of retribution was despatched to the editor of *Adventure*.

The story had the same homing instinct as its predecessors. It came back. But instead of carrying a rejection slip, it returned with a letter and a long page of comments from Editor Arthur Sullivant Hoffman. The letter allowed that I had some detectable ability as a wordsmith and suggested that Mr.

Hoffman would be willing to look at another story. This cheered me immensely.

The page of comments, however, dissected the yarn paragraph by paragraph, even line by line in some passages. Although the story was short, Mr. Hoffman gave it a thorough going over. In one page he managed to compress the essence of an entire course in the writing of commercial fiction. The burden of his complaint was that I knew practically nothing about the business of telling a story. This depressed me so deeply that it seemed there was no other course but to go out and take a walk. A long one, straight into the lake. Although after I read the letter over a few times, I realized that this was advice with a value beyond rubies. Mr. Hoffman was a man who knew, an editor moreover who wasn't above taking time out to give a hand to a beginner who needed help. What he had done, simply, was to save this beginner about two years of trial and error.

The stupidity of a novice writer can be unbelievable. The tale of the fugitive on the slag dump hadn't been aimed at *Adventure* as a logical target; it was a shot in the dark because I knew little about the magazine. Now it seemed a sound idea to read a few copies and discover what *Adventure* was all about.

I found out that it was owned by the Butterick Publishing Company which had done such a flourishing business in dress patterns that it branched out into the magazine field. Its standard-bearer was the *Delineator*, a large, glossy monthly highly popular with women in the boondocks who yearned for the latest information from fashion centers, for advice on cooking and home decoration and for wholesome romantic fiction. Paradoxically, the editor for a while was Theodore Dreiser, unfavorably known to the Watch and Ward Society and all decent people as author of such "pornographic" fiction as *Jennie Gerhardt* and *Sister Carrie*. A secondary publication was *Everybody's Magazine*, full of fiction for male and female readers.

The third was *Adventure*, designed for "red-blooded" men. Although it was printed on pulp paper it wasn't a pulp magazine in content but was, in fact, a respectable journal which boasted a list of high-quality contributors. T.S. Stribling, who went on to win a Pulitzer Prize for fiction, was one of the cover names, as were Rafael Sabatini, Talbot Mundy, Alan LeMay, Gordon Young, H. Bedford-Jones and other skilled craftsmen now forgotten. A writer who shouldered his way into that crowd could feel that he had arrived in professional company. Not up there with Kipling, Conrad or Stephen Crane, perhaps, but with artisans of no mean talent just the same.

A study of the magazine revealed that each author had staked out territory of his own: Sabatini wrote historical swashbuckling romances; Mundy, a sort of junior Kipling, wrote about India and derring-do in Afghanistan; LeMay concerned himself with the American west of frontier days. The deep south was Stribling country; a French writer, George Surdez, dealt with northern Africa and the Foreign Legion. And every one of them wrote with vivid knowledge of his territory. Mundy's India was no phony stage setting; you were sure he had been there, that he had seen it, heard it, smelt it. LeMay's cattlemen and sodbusters had an aroma of honest sweat.

Adventure's world was a male world. Women weren't exactly banned, apparently, but they were seldom visible. When they did appear, they kept to their place, well in the background. On no account did a male ever display any sexual interest in them. Their children, if any, were conceived by some mystical process of osmosis. This attitude prevailed in all publications designed for male readers of that time, in stark contrast to the so-called men's magazines of today.

After grasping *Adventure's* slant, my next step was clearly indicated: another story, and a longer one this time because it was just plain foolish to waste an idea on a 5,000-word yarn when by taking a little trouble I could use 15,000 words and earn three times the money. It would be a story with a Canadian setting, preferably the North Country, with a lot of snow and sub-zero weather. And, it went without saying, no women. This wouldn't be easy because girls were very important to me; but if that was the way *Adventure* wanted it, that was the way it would have to be.

A Mounted Police corporal who had served at a northern outpost once told me about a diligent fellow running a company post who was given a hard time by an independent operator who snuck into his territory and relieved the Indians of their furs before the company man could do it himself. The situation seemed to hold all the elements of a surefire *Adventure* story.

The company man would be the hero. He had to be. And the free trader would be the villain. It stood to reason; he was an evil man because he had no scruples about breaking the rules under which the good company trader operated. It never occurred to me that these rules might bear a little scrutiny. All rules were automatically good rules and the man who obeyed them was automatically a Good Guy. The man who broke the rules was just as automatically a Bay Guy. It was as simple as that.

The hero was christened Hugh Munroe, a Scottish name and therefore indicative of virtue. There are no Scottish villains. Any writer who bestows a Scottish name on his villain, through sheer whimsicality or a mistaken notion that it might be an original thing to do, soon learns that this just doesn't work. It merely confuses the reader.

The Bad Guy, for no good reason that I can recall, was given the name of Joe Moon, which had sinister implications only because it was a little uncommon. An experienced writer would have been more forthright. When you're dealing with poison you don't fool around with fancy labels. Subsequently I learned to give my Bad Guys names such as Vasiliev or Karoski, which being foreign stamped them unmistakably as low characters capable of any knavery.

It never even occurred to me that Trader Munroe, busily engaged in conning the Indians out of their furs under the shelter of the Establishment and screaming "Foul" when independent Joe Moon showed guts enough to muscle in on his racket, was actually the Bad Guy. In fact if there were any Good

Guys around at all, clearly they were the hapless redskins. If this had dawned on me, it wouldn't have made any difference anyway. I may have lacked the rudiments of a social conscience but at least I knew that no popular magazine editor of that day would go for a Good Guy who wasn't a white man. Not even if he said "How" instead of "Massa."

So I sat down and hammered out the story over a period of a couple of weeks, the story of how good Trader Munroe — who had only the interests of the Indians at heart — fought to save his little flock from the rascalities of Joe Moon. There was lots of snow, even a blizzard, and below-zero weather prevailed. Wolves howled by night. The hero fell through a hole in the ice, got his matches wet and nearly froze to death. He had a rough time before he put the free trader to route and got the company's fur business back on its feet.

I titled it "The River Trail," mailed it to *Adventure* and awaited the congratulations of Mr. Hoffman.

I could imagine the comments already. "A new voice in adventure fiction"... "brings the Canadian Northland alive"..."stirring tale of rivalry among the Northern fur traders"..."gripping" ..."better than Jack London."

The story came back in a week. This time Mr. Hoffman's paragraph-by-paragraph, line-by-line critique went on for two pages, and it amounted to another lesson in the writing of popular fiction. My Good Guy solved his problems too easily, largely because the Bad Guy was just plain stupid. Mr. Hoffman pointed out that the villain should be just as smart as the hero, if not smarter. His ruthlessness and lack of scruples should give him an advantage over the hero, who is handicapped by a civilized code of conduct. In short, while it is permissible for the villain to kick the hero in the balls, it is a gross breach of fiction etiquette if the hero reacts accordingly. He is allowed only a straight left to the jaw.

Mr. Hoffman also suggested that the Bad Guy should be ahead most of the way, right up the last chapter if possible. If you can postpone the Good Guy's ultimate triumph to the middle of the last chapter you have it made. You keep piling troubles on him, perhaps letting him come up for breath once in a while, until it appears that he has no possible chance of survival. Then, and not until then, he turns the tables, demolishes the Bad Guy and all his works, and emerges from the wreckage battered but triumphant.

A few years later an old pro, Frank L. Packard, put it to me in simpler terms: "You get your hero into a hole, and then you throw rocks at him." Mr. Packard didn't claim copyright on this recipe; he said he got it from an editor.

Mr. Hoffman did more than comment on the total scheme of the story. He remarked on some passages of flowery writing, of which I was very proud, and recommended that they be tossed out. They slowed down the narrative. He also pointed out that it seemed highly improbable that my Good Guy could fall through the ice of a frozen river — especially when I had insisted that the temperature had been around the zero mark for weeks.

This detail had, in fact, bothered me a little but it was necessary to the plot so I had gone ahead anyway, hoping no one would notice. Mr. Hoffman said editors always noticed things like that. It was part of their job. If an editor slipped up he would soon hear from dozens of eagle-eyed readers anxious to show off. It was up to the author to make every detail airtight.

But there was a note of hope. "If you find these suggestions helpful and if you care to revise the story we'll be glad to look at it again."

I went back to work again on a complete rewrite. The story began to sit up and look remarkably healthy until the Good Guy fell through the ice and there the story stalled. The problem seemed insoluble and yet he had to fall through the ice if the rest of the story was to make any sense. I pondered the problem until my head ached — no solution came.

I paddled up to Sudbury in the canoe, bought a bottle of Scotch and called on a gentle old codger named Page who was said to know the wilderness like the back of his hand. He had gone out with survey parties, worked in lumber camps, gone prospecting, guided hunters and anglers and, "If it warn't for this here goddamn arthritis you wouldn't have found me sitting out on the goddamn veranda on a goddamn pretty day like this, no sir.

"Story writer, hey? Well, my boy, you sure come to the right man. Many's a time I been told I oughta write a book on the story of my life. Yes sir, I can tell you stories you wouldn't believe. I can remember a time once on the Lightning River, it was deer season and I took out this party of goddamn Americans not a one of them could hit a bull's ass with a shovel. . . ."

Mr. Page was halfway through his life story and more than halfway through the bottle before I could divert the conversation onto the subject of winter travel in the wilderness and then he opined that this here goddamn idiot who fell through the ice couldn't have been any too goddamn bright in the first place and his dogs must have been even stupider. "You take a trail dog, he can smell trouble. He's not going out onto bad ice. He don't want to get hisself drownded."

"Where would you find thin ice in the middle of winter?"

"Fast water don't freeze good. Around rapids and falls you gotta watch it. But hell, this guy you're telling me about he must have been a real halfwit. No excuse for going through the ice. Unless," Mr. Page added thoughtfully, "unless he was a goddamn American. Must have been an American. Never met one yet was worth a pinch of dried coonshit in the bush. And you say this idiot found an empty cabin and near froze to death because he couldn't light a fire account of his matches bein' wet?"

"That was the situation."

"He wouldn't have just near froze to death. He would have froze so solid an undertaker couldn't have straightened him out with a hammer. Serve him right too for letting his matches get wet. Any damn fool knows you keep your matches in a watertight tinbox."

I began to realize that I couldn't allow my Good Guy to fall through the ice and get his matches wet. Not if he were to hold the respect of any knowledgeable reader.

"Tell you what," said Mr. Page, "you just fix it so this muttonhead turns out to be an American. Then it won't matter how goddamn stupid he is in the bush. Everybody will say it figures. True to life."

"You don't seem to have a very high opinion of Americans, Mr. Page."

"I didn't say that. Goddamn nice fellows, some of 'em. As long as they stay out of the bush." He took another shot, straight, strangled briefly and wiped the tears from his eyes. "Do I look like a moose?" he inquired.

"Of course not."

"An American mistook me for a moose once. I was guidin' him. Shot me right in the foot. So maybe I'm prejudiced."

I headed back home, deeply depressed. My career had suffered a severe setback just when it seemed to be glowing with promise. The story would have to be junked. I couldn't have a Good Guy who conducted himself, as Mr. Page put it, like a real halfwit, an idiot, a muttonhead and a goddamn fool unless I explained it all by making him an American, which was not calculated to enthuse an American editor.

Then came a blinding revelation.

The Bad Guy would fall through the ice. The Bad Guy, who thought he was smarter than his own dogs and went on ahead of them when they balked, would get dunked for his obstinacy. He had to be the one who didn't know enough to keep his matches in a waterproof box. And it would be the Good Guy who would track him to the cabin just as he was slowly turning into a human icicle.

"For God's sake, Munroe, can't you see I'll freeze to death unless you light a fire. Haven't you got a match?"

"I always have matches, Joe Moon. I keep them in this little waterproof box. They light up like this, see." Then the Good Guy calmly blows out the match.

The Bad Guys utters a shriek of despair. "You can't stand there and watch me freeze. I'm getting pneumonia already. Light the fire."

"I'll light the fire, Joe Moon. But only if you agree to my conditions."

"Anything. Anything!" says Joe Moon, through chattering teeth.

"First, you will hand over those furs you got from my Indians at the cost of a few bottles of rotgut whiskey. And then, Joe Moon, then you will leave the Missabi country forever."

Even Paul, when he got the message on the road to Damascus, couldn't have been more elated. It is more than probable that I broke the Canadian paddling record (singles) getting back to the cottage. After clattering on the typewriter for a while, I sent "The River Trail" out again—and this time it stayed out. Mr. Hoffman accepted it and wrote that he was looking forward to seeing another story. More to the point, his letter was followed by a check for $300.

CHAPTER 14:

Literature for the Growing Child

The first big sale can be an accident. The second can be a coincidence. But when Hoffman bought half a dozen more stories in rapid order, I felt I was on my way to fortune. When Dinehart showed interest in "Imposter," I was sure of it. That was why I crossed the border to become a Broadway playwright, arrived in Springfield and made the Stratemeyer connection which sent me back to the wilderness cabin until the Autumn gales blew me back to Haileybury as Franklin W. Dixon.

Now the wheel had come full circle, and I was home again. But since the fire everything had changed. The Grand Theatre was gone. The bank was gone. The lake boats were gone with the plank sidewalks and the lockup. The hotels were gone with their mahogany bars and paintings of voluptuous women. Instead I found a forward-looking community with brand-new buildings and nothing old about it anywhere. It even had a Lions Club. The place oozed respectability.

My father now presided over a fine new school with all modern improvements, but even at fifty-five he was beginning to look tired. He had had a nerve-wracking career as a teacher, yet he could still glow with pleasure when some bright kid with curiosity and a lively mind showed up in his class in September. And he could still regard some slack-jawed lunkhead as a challenge. In fact, the most dismal lunkheads often aroused his greatest affection because he knew they needed him most. The bright ones would manage regardless, but the natural dolts — who would nowadays be classified as "under-achievers" to make everyone feel better — were the ones who had to be helped. Somehow he would always send them up to the annual examinations for entrance into high school with enough knowledge in their befuddled skulls to get them through. That done, come another September, there would be another class and the treadmill began all over again.

It had begun to tell. I thought of the stories he had told me of himself as a sixteen-year-old farm lad who coped with forty boys and girls of all ages, some older than himself, in one-room school houses for an annual wage of $250. Every year he would move on to another school in another Ottawa Valley village. I thought, too, of the pretty, brown-eyed girl with whom he fell in love when he boarded at the cooper's house in a tiny village called Clayton and whom he married when he achieved his first big school in a real town — Carleton Place, population 2,000. She had accepted the genteel poverty of a teacher's life in a day when everyone respected the schoolmaster and the trust-ees underpaid him so scandalously that it was hard for him to maintain self-respect. Most of the burden of stretching scarce dollars had fallen on her shoulders, yet I always recall her as cheerful and singing. And because she was cheerful we were all cheerful; I remember my childhood as a happy time. I can recall my father's bookcase with its leather-bound one-volume editions of Longfellow, Milton, Tennyson, Wordsworth and Shakespeare. He had a deep affection for poetry, which I was unable to share, but I fell upon the *Complete Works of Charles Dickens* with absolute joy the day the set arrived in the house. Those red-bound volumes introduced me to a world of imagi-nation and magic that can be evoked by a master. Dickens and an Empire typewriter which my father bought at about the same time resolved my future. He seldom used the typewriter himself, but neither encouraged nor discouraged its use by his boys. So I used it, learning by trial and error with two fingers.

I realize now, of course, that by today's standards any kid

bought up in a remote northern town during the second decade of this century was underprivileged. It was a good thing that we didn't know it. We didn't know the boon of organized recreation. In summer we could play ball in a lumpy vacant lot (without a certified coach to show us how and a gallery of howling parents to inspire us), go swimming in a lake frigid enough to turn us blue in five minutes. In winter we could play a scrambly kind of hockey—about twenty youngsters to a side —on a backyard rink bordered by snowbanks. In the light of the superior advantages enjoyed by young athletes of today's Little Leagues, it is clear that we grew up under such wretched conditions that I can't understand why it seemed to me that we had such a hell of a lot of fun. We just didn't know any better.

Lacking the technological blessings that make the lives of children in the Blackmail Age so rich in entertainment, we somehow managed to survive an existence which must have been inexpressibly dreary but which I delude myself into remembering as a golden time. Maybe just being a kid was enough.

We had no stereos or record players, of course. Nearly every household had a primitive gramophone which had to be wound up by a crank. We had a selection of a dozen records which came with the machine and were played over and over. "Cohen on the Telephone" was pretty hilarious until young listeners found themselves beating Cohen to the punchlines.

Radio was a device useful only to ships at sea, and of passing interest to youth because it helped a Scotland Yard inspector clap the handcuffs on the unhappy Dr. Crippen who did his wife in and fled from England on an ocean liner equipped with a wireless. This taught us the wisdom of keeping up with scientific developments.

Television was merely an idea in the head of a frustrated German named Lipkow, cursing a *verdamt* scanning machine that wouldn't work because he couldn't figure out how to invent the phototube.

Movies we had, but they were pretty crude—nothing like the sound-and-color entertainments so valuable in educating today's youngsters in the arts of robbery and rape, sodomy and seduction, mayhem and murder. For a few hours at the Grand Theatre every Saturday afternoon, in a silence shattered only by a jangling piano and our own happy shrieks, we managed to put up with the perilous adventures of Pearl White, Eddie Polo and Grace Cunard and the buffooneries of Ham and Bud, Fatty Arbuckle and Charlie Chaplin before someone told him he was a genius.

So, with time on our hands, we read.

To compensate for our dismal lack of other entertainment, there was a copious supply of reading matter — admittedly uncertified, unpasteurized and probably unhealthy — easily available to the growing boy. At Christmas every normal Canadian lad felt neglected if he failed to receive a five-pound volume of either *The Boys' Own Annual* or *Chums*. These were the collected numbers of two weekly magazines for boys, published in England and bound annually in hard covers for export to the colonies. With pen and ink illustrations, printed in 1,000 pages of eyestraining type, they were packed with fiction calculated to brighten the most monotonous juvenile existence.

Each had its devout worshippers. If a youngster's folks were of British origin, he got *The Boys' Own*, which was an institution so venerable that many lads assumed that King Alfred read it as a child. If the kid's parents were Canadian-born, he got *Chums*, snooted by connoisseurs of things British as a base imitation of *The Boys' Own*, fit only for colonials with no respect for tradition. Either way, the lucky lad found enough wholesome reading in these prodigious volumes to keep him going until the next Christmas.

The serials alone were worth the price of admission because they represented a dozen full-length books, with the extra advantage that you didn't have to wait a week between instalments but could devour them at one lusty gulp. Some of these serials dealt with public school life in England—a life so jolly, so packed with highjinks, so dedicated to fun and games, so gloriously free of study, homework and parental authority that we went around envying the normal British schoolboy as fortune's favored son. Others concerned clean-cut English lads who never, apparently, went to school at all, but spent their youth battling savage tribes in Africa and India or ranging through history as they took on pirates on the Spanish Main, nihilists in darkest Russia, highwaymen in Merrie England or Vikings in ancient Britain. Invariably they encountered the gravest perils; invariably they emerged triumphant. Invariably, too, British imperialism was portrayed in a highly favorable light as a boon to everybody, including any misguided natives who got slaughtered along the way.

By way of international balance we had imports from the U.S.A. such as the Alger books, the Rover Boys and Frank Merriwell, a clean-living American boy who excelled at every sport devised by man, from tiddlywinks to polo. Frank was exceptionally clean. In fact, all this literature put a high premium on clean living, which confused us a lot because we were never quite sure what it meant. Clean living was never actually spelled out. Obviously it meant using your toothbrush every day and washing your feet every week, but we knew it couldn't be that simple. We had an uneasy feeling that it also meant giving up masturbation but the books didn't say.

Clean living or not, under these literary influences the Canadian boy grew up in a state of proper humility. His reading taught him that British boys were courageous, daring, ingenious and always in the right so that they always came out on top while, incidentally, having more fun than anyone. At the same time his reading taught him that American boys were likewise courageous, daring and ingenious and, moreover, so devoted to honest toil that they always wound up rich. Canadian boys, who apparently had no history worth writing about and no forebears who ever made it as heroes of books, were clearly made of inferior stuff. This probably explains why the adult, male Canadian today is a docile, modest fellow who knows his place and is never given to throwing his weight around.

Granted that the British influence was strong, the American influence was stronger. The jut-jawed heroes of *Chums* were admirable chaps all right, but they spoke a strange language full of obscure references to "pater" and "mater" and exclamatory remarks such as "I say, old boy!" and "Jolly good!" They were also given to performing their heroics in the damndest places, such as the jungles of Madagascar or the Sargasso Sea. The Alger books, on the other hand, presented boys who spoke understandable English and who engaged in recognizable occupations such as raising turnips or selling papers. They followed these humble careers in familiar places, on farms or city street corners or even on trains. In short, our kind of people. As models of conduct their influence was formidable — up to a point. Even after an Alger book we went right on detesting work and hoping that by some miracle we would get rich anyway.

The Alger books had another virtue. They were cheap. Most of them were paperbacks and cost a dime. True, they were obtainable in hardcover editions and, occasionally, an aunt who didn't know the facts of life would come across with one of these volumes as a birthday gift. But it seemed wasteful. A paperback, after perusal, could easily be traded for another. Theoretically, it was possible for a diligent boy with a large circle of friends to read *all* the Alger books for an initial investment of ten cents. None of us ever achieved this feat, but we tried.

Frank Merriwell was even cheaper. He cost only a nickel in a tabloid-size paper "The Tip Top Weekly" with a front-page illustration in red, blue and yellow. Sixteen pages of dense type. Wish fulfilment for every red-blooded boy. Every week, too. Back numbers available from Street and Smith, Publishers, every copy eulogizing next week's adventure. We also had a choice of two titles, such as "Frank Merriwell's Winning Touchdown" or "The Kidnapped Quarterback." You got your nickel's worth.

I was always fond of Frank Merriwell but when I discovered that I had permanently stopped growing, my admiration turned to idolatry. To a stumble-footed youngster who always misjudged the fly ball, who made the hockey team only because he owned the puck and who couldn't even finish third in the annual Sunday School picnic sack race, it was inspiring to share, however vicariously, the triumphs of an athlete who always won. Frank was merely the world's most versatile athlete. He was not just good at games; he was a superstar in every sport. As a baseball pitcher, he relied on a baffling double curve which was good for a no-hit, no-run game whenever his arm was right and the umpires were honest. If a teammate fell ill or was abducted by unscrupulous opponents, Frank could fill in behind the plate, in outfield or infield and could be counted on to play errorless ball and bat his usual .500. As a quarterback, his eighty-yard pass for the winning touchdown in the final second of play was as certain as sunset. In track, he could win at any height or distance, with or without a broken leg. Rowing, lacrosse, hockey, automobile racing, cycling, swimming—just name the sport and Frank Merriwell was your boy, a guaranteed winner in the next-to-closing paragraph each and every week.

The Frank Merriwell stories were written by Gilbert Patten, who began writing pulp fiction when he was sixteen and was asked to tackle the new series for Street and Smith in 1896 after an apprenticeship of about a dozen years. Frank Merriwell broke new ground so successfully that Patten turned out a story complete in one issue every week for the next two decades, under the house name of Burt L. Standish.

Technically, Burt was still alive in the late Thirties, as I have good reason to remember. One of the shining moments of my life came in 1937 when Street and Smith ran two of my stories in one magazine. This meant that one called for use of a house name and I discovered that I had become, for the moment, Burt L. Standish. Such eminence does not come to everyone.

It might seem that the redoubtable Patten was the most prolific author in the history of the world. Anyone capable of writing an original 30,000-word story every week for more than twenty years has got to be right up there. However, another Street and Smith writer, Frederick Van Rensselaer Dey, whacked out a Nick Carter novel for the "Nick Carter Weekly" for seventeen years, and Lester Dent, writing under the house name of Kenneth Robeson, wrote 60,000 words a month for the Doc Savage magazine over a fifteen-year period. He was a mere dawdler, however, compared to the incredible Frederick Faust, who worked under half a dozen names of which Max Brand was the best known. The gigantic Faust — he was six feet, three—began in Westerns and wrote entire issues of pulp magazines at the rate of 10,000 words a day, went on to write for better magazines and turned out 200 books in a quarter of a century. He was one of the few writers who worked at this top capacity when full of booze. Known to his intimates as "Heinie," he was killed in Italy in 1944 while serving as a war correspondent. After years at a desk creating imaginary adventures for imaginary people, he felt he was entitled to something real for himself.

For sheer volume it is unlikely that anyone ever equalled Frank Richards who wrote a 30,000-word story, the entire contents of *Magnet*, an English magazine for boys, every week for thirty years. Early in the century Richards created an imaginary public school for boys, called it Greyfriars, bestowed upon it a fat pupil called Billy Bunter and went on from there to make Billy Bunter one of the best-known characters in English fiction. Richards never denied that Billy Bunter derived from Dickens' fat boy, but he always insisted that he had done what few other writers had ever been able to do — he breathed life into Billy Bunter.

Billy Bunter was no hero. He was a sneak, a glutton and a troublemaker and he fascinated every young reader who ever encountered him. Mr. Richards was merely following some well-established precedents. Who is Shakespeare's most memorable character? Falstaff—a lecherous, cowardly, lying, old drunkard. Dickens'? Wilkins Micawber, deadbeat and blowhard. One could compile a formidable list, all the way through Becky Sharp and Long John Silver to Mr. Glencannon.

George Orwell, who was fascinated by what he called "good bad books," wrote a learned essay in which he expressed doubt that Frank Richards wrote all the *Magnet* stories, and faulted the yarns because they made fun of foreigners, especially Frenchmen. Because the series could not have been written by one person, he said, it followed that they had to be written "in a style easily imitated."

Back came a tough reply from Mr. Richards, who happened to be alive and kicking. He kicked hard. He declared that he had indeed written all the stories all by himself. As for the style, "whatever its merits or demerits, it is my own and—if I may say it with due modesty—inimitable." As for Billy Bunter, "Shaw, Ibsen and Chekhov couldn't make a character live like Billy Bunter. Only the born storyteller can do it. Shakespeare could do it and so could Dickens but Thackeray and Scott couldn't."

The fluent Richards, now in full spate, concluded: "As for foreigners being funny, I must shock Mr. Orwell by telling him that foreigners *are* funny. They lack the sense of humor which is the special gift of our own chosen nation."

Just to nail down Mr. Richard's claim to the all-time heavyweight title, it should be noted that his championship doesn't rest on his feats of wordage for *Magnet* alone. The only rival to *Magnet* was a weekly paper for boys called *Gem*, about lively didoes at another boys' school named St. Jim's, penned with unflagging zest and regularity by one Martin Clifford. Admirers of *Magnet* and Greyfriars often debated hotly with fans of *Gem* and St. Jim's over the respective merits of Authors Richards and Clifford. These disputes ended with the incredible revelation that Frank Richards was also Martin Clifford. Those who claim to know will tell you that all writers of vast output were hacks who proved that prodigious wordage is always equated with total lack of talent. This does not necessarily follow. There is a flaw in the argument. Charles Dickens was a wordsmith who turned out a staggering amount of material while meeting monthly deadlines year after year. His facility was eclipsed only by his ability to breathe life into memorable characters in pretty distinctive prose. I rest my case.

There were, of course, books of another kind — forbidden books.

Not pornography. *Fannie Hill* never came our way. We were, as I have already noted, underprivileged, deprived of many of the educational opportunities enjoyed by the kids of today. Occasionally, it must be admitted, something juicy showed up from mysterious sources, typed on flimsy paper and passed from hand to hand with great caution. Only God could help anyone caught with one of these missives. We were pretty sure God would not be inclined to intervene.

My younger brother Frank received one of these missives in class one day, hastily conveyed to him by a schoolmate who didn't care to retain it a moment longer than necessary. He had just read the first verse — a poem concerning the amatory adventures of a stenographer — when the teacher pounced. "Give me that!" she commanded.

From the one verse my brother gathered that the poem was not one of Longfellow's works. It was enough to convince him that if the teacher cast eyes on it, he would be kicked out of school as a starter, then probably sent to jail and perhaps even shot. There was only one way to dispose of the damning evidence. He ate it.

He claims he has never been able to stomach off-color literature since. In any case he escaped scot-free, and even enjoyed considerable distinction for the next twenty-four hours as the only kid in school whose digestive organs were lined with wall-to-wall pornography. He even hiccupped in an obscene sort of way.

Our forbidden books were of a different nature. They were called dime novels.

There was some confusion about the genre. A Frank Merriwell looked like a midget newspaper and cost only a nickel, so obviously it wasn't a dime novel and thus escaped censure. And an Alger book, which looked like a novel and cost a dime, was somehow respectable. On the other hand, you possessed a copy of *Jesse James on the Hoodoo Trail* at your peril. And *Trapped in a Tong War* by Nick Carter, Jr. was the sort of book a lad perused in the privy if he knew what was good for him.

Those were dime novels. And dime novels were sinful. Whenever our clergyman inveighed against the iniquities of the time and warned against the evils which beset the young, he usually began with all-out onslaught against cigarettes, moved on to a wholesale condemnation of cards, dancing, movies and booze, then wound up with a blistering denunciation of poisonous reading matter known as dime novels.

We found it puzzling that the iniquity seemed to be determined by cash outlay. Obviously Jesse James was beyond the pale because everyone knew Jesse went around for a long while with a price on his head until he got his come-uppance from Frankie Howard. But Nick Carter was a detective, on the side of the law. So why was it that a Nick Carter paperback, discovered under one's pillow, brought the same punishment, with the offending volume consigned to the fire, as a Jesse James book? The answer was simple. They were dime novels.

Today when a lad concludes that his parents are irrational, that his teachers contradict themselves and that his pastor — if he has one — is irrelevant, his course of conduct is clear. He renounces baths and barbers, sets fire to the schoolhouse and pickets the House of God. In our time this kind of active protest was unthinkable; retribution would have been swift and calamitous. The authorities, meaning anyone over thirty, were always right, even when they were transparently wrong. If it was sinful to smoke, swear, go swimming on the Sabbath, venture into the shrubbery with a curious maiden or read dime novels, it was doubly sinful to question our elders. So we shrugged resignedly in the face of our mystifying universe and went on readying our Alger books, grateful that they at least had achieved sanctity.

There were books for girls, too, notably the Elsie Books, but a lad would sooner be caught with a forbidden copy of Eugene Field's *Only a Boy* in his possession than with an Elsie Book. A good deal sooner, in fact, even if *Only a Boy* meant a fate just short of being skinned alive. At least he would have enjoyed some lusty reading, although nowadays Mr. Field's chronicle of sexual initiation would be regarded as pretty pallid stuff.

There was a long shelf of Elsie Books, all perpetrated by a lady named Farquharson who got her start, like Horatio Alger, by writing for Sunday school publications. She used the alias of Martha Finley.

One summer I spent several weeks at the home of a girl cousin who was addicted to Elsie Books. The household had little more by way of printed matter and as I was one of those compulsive readers who would tackle *The Home Veterinarian's Guide* if there was nothing else around, I consumed six entire volumes of the Elsie series from cover to cover. It is unlikely that any other boy in the whole world has ever managed this feat and survived. The experience left me shaken, but at least I am in a privileged position to testify that in the Himalayas of junk turned out by writers of juvenile fiction the Elsie Books stand like Everest as the worst ever written by anybody, and that Elsie Dinsmore is without peer the Most Nauseating Heroine of all time.

The extraordinary feature of Elsie's enormous popularity (she won the solemn approval of parents and Sunday school superintendents alike) lay in the fact that these godly volumes were simply loaded with implications of incest. Apparently the parents and Sunday school superintendents never read them or, if they did, were too insensitive to recognize an incestous situation when they stumbled over it. Perhaps it was because the reciprocal adoration of Elsie Dinsmore and her jealous Papa was coated with a syrupy goo of Biblical quotations. Anyhow, it says something for the innocence of the age.

Elsie was the only daughter of a widowed plantation owner who spent most of his time demanding proof of Elsie's undivided love for him and sending her to bed for all kinds of domestic transgressions. Mr. Dinsmore was such a sadistic bastard burdened by so many nasty complexes that even Freud would have kicked him off of the couch. Whenever Dinsmore punished his daughter, which happened in every other chapter, Elsie was so prostrated by the conviction that Papa didn't return her affection for him that she just wanted to die.

One such emotional crisis occupied the greater part of a whole book when Dinsmore subjected Elsie to a ten-page inquisition as to the real depth of her love for him, and she confessed that she loved her Heavenly Father even more than she loved her Papa. When she stubbornly refused to recant because she was afraid she would go to hell if she put God second (although insisting that it was practically a photo finish), Dismore was so consumed by jealousy that he wouldn't speak to her for a month.

I doubt if Mrs. Farquharson ever suspected, but they *must* have been sleeping together.

The Elsie Books were unique in that the major characters became older, book by book. I know of no other juvenile series in which this happened. Frank Merriwell was born in prep school and went on to Yale, but I don't think he ever graduated. Probably abnormally slow, even for a letter-man. But Jack Harkaway, Tom Swift, the Rover Boys and certainly the Hardy brothers never grew up. Alger heroes, of course, enjoyed lives of no more than 200 pages.

Mrs. Farquharson probably lived to regret this policy because after half a dozen volumes Little Elsie just naturally became a teenager. It then became clear that the great romance with Papa couldn't go on much longer without becoming a little conspicuous, if not suspect and eligible to be banned in Boston. The solution at this stage was to invent a handsome young man who paid court to the nubile Elsie. I saw nothing wrong with the chap, beyond the evidence that anyone who wanted to marry Elsie Dinsmore was obviously a candidate for institutional care, but characters have a way of taking over a book and Mr. Dinsmore had to stay in character.

He was so jealous of the suitor, who proved to be equipped with more than the normal complement of guts in defying the monster, that he set out to expose the rascal as a fortune hunter, and succeeded. Faithful readers must have greeted this triumph with mixed feelings. After all, Elsie Dinsmore was *human*, wasn't she? Or was she? In any case, the reprobate was sent packing and the grateful Elsie was snuggling up to Papa again in the final chapter.

After buying the next book and discovering that Elsie's comfy little domestic romance was destined to go on forever, the Elsie fans apparently became a little restive. Perhaps sales fell off. Mrs. Farquharson had to come up with something. So she trotted out another suitor. And who did he turn out to be? Why none other than Dinsmore's bosom pal, Mr. Travilla, who had been wandering in and out of every book as the Old Family Friend!

Eligible? Even Dinsmore couldn't fault him. Not only was Mr. Travilla the same age as Dinsmore, he was just as rich, just as unwed, just as godly and he also owned a plantation. Practically a carbon copy of Elsie's father. In short, a candidate of impeccable credentials. The Travilla-Dinsmore nuptials were duly celebrated in half a dozen chapters of ecstatic prose, with overtones of celestial choirs hymning the event, and if Elsie absentmindedly moaned "Oh, Papa!" during the conjugal embraces, Mr. Travilla shouldn't have been at all surprised.

Mrs. Farquharson, getting her second wind, was able to go on and on to such books as *Elsie's Children* and *Elsie's Widowhood* (Travilla apparently couldn't stand the pace at his age) and even to *Grandmother Elsie* for her loyal and also aging public.

One of my prized possessions, which I discovered in the well named Old Favorites Book Shop in Toronto, is a copy of *Elsie's Holidays at Roseland*, one of the pre-wedding volumes. When Mrs. Farquharson finished writing a book she did not, apparently, fool around building up her energies for the next one. She merely spat on her hands in a ladylike way and kept right on going without a break in the action. Bemused readers who came upon an Elsie Book for the first time would have to rush out and buy the immediately preceding volume if they wanted to know what the hell was going on. Accordingly, *Elsie's Holidays at Roseland* begins in full flight.

> *Elsie felt in better spirits in the morning; her sleep had refreshed her, and she arose with a stronger confidence in the love of both her earthly and her heavenly father.*

She found her papa ready and waiting for her. He took her in his arms and kissed her tenderly. "My precious little daughter," he said, "papa is very glad to see you looking so bright and cheerful this morning. I think something was wrong with my little girl last night. Why did she not come to papa with her trouble?"

The trouble concerned, of all things, "a trashy book" which had fallen into Elsie's hands through no fault of her own. The vigilant Dinsmore had condemned this book as injurious to the young. Naturally he had no alternative but to banish Elsie from the previous evening's dinner table. (Elsie missed an average of a dozen meals per volume.)

Now, if we are to judge from Dinsmore's solicitous inquiries, all is forgiven. And because papa is always right, Elsie bears no ill will. In fact she doesn't even ask what happened to breakfast. Instead, she assures her parent that she wouldn't think of reading any book that failed to meet his approval.

"This is my own darling child," said he, returning her caress. "Your ready obedience deserves a reward. Now put on your hat and we will take a walk."

Mr. Travilla joined them in the avenue, and his kind heart rejoiced to see how all the clouds of care and sorrow had passed away from his little friend's face, leaving it bright and beaming as usual. Her father had one hand and Mr. Travilla soon possessed himself of the other.

"What do you say, Travilla, to a ride on horseback with the young ladies and myself?"

"Bravo! I shall be delighted to be of the party if the ladies don't object; eh, Elsie, what do you think?" with a questioning look down into her glad face. "Will they want me?"

"You needn't be a bit afraid, Mr. Travilla," laughed the little girl. "I like you next to papa and I believe the other girls like you better."

"Oh take care, Elsie; are you not afraid of hurting your father's feelings?"

"No danger, as long as she puts me first," Mr. Dinsmore said, bestowing a smile and loving glance on her.

This is about all we really need to know about Little Elsie and her elderly admirers—papa with his Jehovah complex and Mr. Travilla with his predeliction for nymphets.

One reason *Elsie's Holidays at Roseland* ranks high on my list of unforgettable books is because it is the only work of fiction, to my knowledge, in which the heroine dies and achieves a glorious resurrection. That's right. In Chapter Twelve of this immortal work, Elsie Dinsmore, in full view of her physician and weeping relatives, passed away.

The trouble began as before, with a book. Apparently the Dinsmores never could see eye to eye on literary matters. The volume had been chosen by Papa, who asked Elsie to read to him on Saturday evening. Come Sunday morning he asked her to resume.

> *The book her father bade her read to him was simply a fictitious tale without a particle of religious truth in it and, Elsie's conscience told her, entirely unfit for Sabbath reading.*

So Elsie said no.

The consequences were horrendous. At first the astonished Dinsmore merely said he had seen ministers reading worse books on Sunday and commanded Elsie to get with it.

Elsie said no again, and Dinsmore became a little riled.

> *"I should be strongly tempted to whip you into submission," he said, "had I the strength to do it."*

The poor man had been laid up for a few days with a fever and lacked even the strength for his favorite indoor recreation.

Elsie still said no. Mr. Dinsmore then held a watch on the recalcitrant child and gave her ten minutes to come across.

At the end of the ten minutes Elsie said no again. After that, of course, there was nothing else for a loving father to do but banish the obstinate kid from his presence, cut off her pocket money and sentence her to solitary confinement in her room on a bread-and-water diet. Then, no end upset, he went off on a much needed vacation to recuperate.

Elsie had her revenge, however. After several weeks of

punishment, all the while stubbornly insisting that she would read the offensive volume to her father on any other day of the week but never on Sunday, she lost weight and color, and finally came down with brain fever.

Between intervals of delirium she even made her will. It provided for maintenance of a missionary to the heathen and left instructions for her burial "under a plain white stone with a verse of Scripture." This was enough for Mr. Travilla's mother, who was pinch-hitting as housekeeper. She decided that this was more than an ordinary case of female obstinacy. She sent for Dinsmore.

When the fond father returned home and was told that Elsie probably wouldn't last the night, he was frantic with contrition.

"Doctor, is there no hope?" he asked in a hoarse whisper.

"Mr. Dinsmore," said the doctor, "I will be frank with you. Had you returned one week ago, even yesterday, she might have been saved. But now I see not one ray of hope."

"My punishment is greater than I can bear," moaned Mr. Dinsmore.

It served the old bastard right. He went to his room to brood and repent. But it did him no good.

The first streak of dawn was beginning in the eastern sky when the doctor, who had been bending over her for several minutes, suddenly laid his finger on her pulse for an instant; then turned to his fellow watchers with a look there was no mistaking.

There was weeping and wailing then in that room, where deathlike stillness had reigned so long.

"Her poor father!" exclaimed Mrs. Travilla.

"I will go to him. I promised to call him the moment she waked and now I must tell him she will never wake again."

"No," replied Mrs. Travilla, "rather tell him she has waked in heaven and is even now singing the song of the redeemed."

Mr. Dinsmore was given the bad news. Then he settled

down to read a pretty lengthy farewell letter Elsie had written on her deathbed. It ran to a good thousand words.

As for Elsie's loyal fans, their consternation can be imagined. Granted that they admired Elsie for standing by her beliefs, they must have felt that Mrs. Farquharson had gone a little too far this time.

Dinsmore was weeping dismally over the farewell letter when there was a knock at the door. He assumed his visitor was the undertaker.

But wait! This is no undertaker. It is the doctor.

"Mr. Dinsmore, are you prepared for good news? Can you bear it, my dear sir?"

Mr. Dinsmore caught at the furniture for support and gasped for breath.

"What is it?" he asked hoarsely.

"Good news, I said. Your child yet lives, and though her life still hangs by a thread the crisis is past and I have some hope that she may recover."

Obviously even doctors who make house calls can make a little mistake once in a while.

And that is why I think *Elsie's Holidays at Roseland* deserves an honored place on any shelf of Great Works of American Humor along with the best of Mark Twain—who worked hard at being funny while Mrs. Farquharson did it without even trying.

These, then, were the books devoured by the young in the early part of this century — the Algers, the Frank Merriwells and the Elsies — the books that molded our characters and helped make us the sterling folk we are today.

CHAPTER 15:

The Man Who Chased Fire Engines

The all-time champion of juvenile output, when all is said and done, however, has to be the Great Horatio.

Alger, that is.

He too wrote books for boys. Hand over fist. Scores of them. And he didn't care who knew it because he was proud of them. He signed his name to most of them, with one little flourish; as an author he insisted upon being known as Horatio Alger, *Junior*.

There didn't seem to be much point to it because Horatio, Senior, was an undistinguished New England clergyman unlikely to be confused with any literary figure alive, but maybe Horatio thought it added a touch of balance, like parting one's hair in the middle. His admirers regarded it as a minor eccentricity of genius along with a few other offbeat manifestations which included an uncontrollable passion for chasing fire engines. Even if he was in the middle of writing a chapter, with a publisher's deadline facing him, if he heard the clang of a firebell he would hurl his pen aside and go sailing out the door in hot pursuit of the galloping horses and crimson fire wagons.

During my boyhood in Haileybury I went through a phase when I was among his devoted admirers. I got over it, of course. We all did. Actually I came in at the tail end of a vast procession of the devout, a procession that had swollen into the millions over half a century. We had one thing in common:

we devoured Alger. We plunked down our money for his books with an enthusiasm seldom matched in the history of publishing.

Why?

It wasn't merely because they were written in a style which was easy to read and easy to understand, with simple words, short paragraphs and shorter sentences narrated almost entirely in dialogue. There were other reasons, but to understand them one would also have to understand the moral climate of North America in the late eighteen-hundreds.

Church steeples studded the land. Holy men, graduated from red-brick academies, preached the divine truths of the Old Testament and threatened eternal damnation from half a million pulpits every Sunday. Any adult who failed to attend church regularly was suspected of unmentionable sins. Every youngster who enjoyed the advantages of "a good home," i.e., a household with a thirty-pound family Bible on the parlor table, attended Sunday school as a matter of course. And it was the institution of the Sunday school that brought about the literary tradition adorned by Horatio Alger and his imitators and disciples.

Gone with the corset, the buttonhook and the medicine show, the Sunday school deserves a nostalgic passage of respect for the benefit of those born too late to endure its torments. It was not peculiar to the nineteenth century; indeed, it was going strong well into the twentieth. I have vivid recollections of Sabbaths in the first decade and of a gentle old grandmother who considered it sinful to preruse any reading matter other than Holy Writ on that day, or to sing, whistle or even hum any melody outside the Methodist Hymnal. No matter how warm the day, a boy who went swimming on Sunday was offending God so grievously that if he were carried home dead by drowning, the general verdict would be that he had it coming.

It was not, in short, a cheerful day. In the morning you scrubbed until your skin glowed; you polished until your boots gleamed; you attired yourself in unaccustomed and uncomfortable garments; you journeyed to a dismal church where your buttocks ached from ninety minutes on an oak pew with a high, hard back, and you listened to a sermon you didn't understand delivered in a threatening voice by a lean, harsh man you didn't like. You raised your piping voice in doleful hymns extolling the therapeutic effects of bathing in blood. Your knees ached while the pastor engaged in a long, intimate conversation with God.

Apparently God couldn't understand plain English because this monologue was studded with thees and thous and thou arts and thou hasts. This was followed by a very long, very dull and damn near incomprehensible sermon which explained how important it was that we love God in spite of a complete lack of evidence that there was a God at all.

Another hymn and you trudged back home for Sunday dinner, the big meal of the week. Stuffed, you were not privileged to sleep it off. It may have been a day of rest for adults; not so for children. Gorged with roast pork and pie, farting and belching, you headed back to the church again and the further agonies of Sunday school. There you studied the dubious legends of the Old Testament and pretended that you actually believed stories that common sense told you were downright lies (such as that ridiculous yarn about Noah and his homemade boat). You were allowed to experience the exquisite joy of sacrifice when you dropped a penny into the pot for the heathen. As you marched past you sang a hymn specially composed for this rite:

Dropping, dropping, dropping, dropping
Hear the pennies fall.
Every one for Jesus.
He will get them all.

There seemed to be a contradiction here. The Superintendent told us the money would buy hymn books for Hottentots but the hymn promised that Jesus would get every cent. In the face of this dilemma, some of us became proficient in dropping slugs and buttons into the bowl while palming our pennies for more useful purposes at the corner store. If Jesus and the Hottentots couldn't get together, there seemed little point in depriving ourselves.

I never knew or heard of a child who actually enjoyed Sunday school. If there was any crumb of consolation, it lay in the knowledge that we were not suffering alone. In dank church basements all over the Christian land, from the Mexican border to the Arctic Circle, from the forests of Vancouver Island to the swamps of the Everglades, youngsters who had never harmed a living soul did penance for imaginary sins by attendance at Sunday school.

The institution was detested so unanimously by youngsters that we found it impossible to understand why it was approved so unanimously by our parents. As we became older the reason became obvious. In the normal Christian household those midafternoon Sunday hours provided the only period of the week in which loving couples had the house entirely to themselves. After two o'clock on a Sabbath afternoon in July the deep and solemn hush that fell over the residential thoroughfares of the small towns of North America was broken only by the happy *twang* that resounded occasionally through open windows up and down the streets as bedsprings joyfully celebrated the precious hours of liberation.

Naturally there were youngsters who sought ways of escape. As a Sunday school employed no truant officer, there seemed no reason why a young sinner couldn't bypass the church and go about his own devices with no one the wiser. It seemed so easy, in fact, that there was bound to be a catch in it.

The catch was that every youngster who attended Sunday school was rewarded with a Sunday school paper. This could be a tiny four-page publication for the little tots, a larger eight-page sheet for the intermediates or a full-fledged sixteen-page magazine for the advanced scholars, complete with a religious puzzle, a moral short story and perhaps even a continued serial guaranteed to be wholesome, uplifting and full of Christian sentiments.

Anyone who failed to return home after Sunday school

without his paper was automatically subject to interrogation. It was a very handy device to ensure high attendance figures. It stood to reason, therefore, that with half a dozen Sunday schools going full blast in every hamlet and village in the land, while thousands flourished in the larger communities, the production of Sunday school literature became a lively part of the American publishing industry. Some denominations, in fact, established their own presses and even competed with old-line publishers by coming up with Spring and Fall fiction lists.

The tales published in the weekly Sunday school magazines conformed to certain elementary standards. Simple words, simple sentences, simple plots and simple characters added up to stories so simple that it appeared as if almost anyone could write them. This was not so, as many a writer learned when he decided to toss off a moral fable for one of these journals and pick up a few easy bucks. This attitude begat failure. A writer must not condescend. You can't write down— not even to tiny tots. Syntax can be improved, spelling can be corrected, construction can be altered, but you can't fake dumb sincerity.

Horatio Alger, son of a New England pastor, had that sincerity and more. He not only wanted to become an author, but apparently he actually admired the stories he read in Sunday school papers and longed to emulate them. Tradition has it, as usual, that he was so poor that he couldn't afford a writing pad so he wrote his first story on brown wrapping paper, with a lead pencil. But if Alger's first editor had a little trouble deciphering Alger's first effort, he was rewarded. His verdict was that the story contained the exact combination of ingredients essential to this humble branch of literature. In the author he detected a mixture of naiveté, earnestness, godliness, simplicity, idiocy and story-telling ability that amounted to genius.

He bought the story and begged for more. Alger had been destined for the ministry but from then on he was an author, and the Alger prose so charmed the captive Sunday school audience that book publishers sniffed it out. The serials became bound volumes. Then Alger's eighth book, *Ragged Dick*, hit the jackpot.

Alger graduated to popular, big-circulation magazines such as Frank Munsey's *Argosy*, and turned out three or four serials a year which book publishers gobbled up until the end of his life. Alger books didn't just sell well. They sold phenomenally. They sold by the million.

Biographers and bibliographers disagree on the number of books Alger wrote and publishers sold, but 125 titles and 400 million copies would be a fair estimate. Ralph D. Gardner, a New York advertising man who has made Algermania his special field of study, makes the flat statement that Horatio Alger was the best-selling author in American history. No one else comes even close.

The fact is that Alger holds two titles, neither open to serious dispute. He wrote and sold more books than anyone else. He was the worst writer who ever lived. There may be a connection. The fact remains that at the turn of the century most American boys firmly believed that Horatio Alger was the greatest author writing in the English language.

Alger had tapped an inexhaustible oilfield. Somehow his little tales exerted a powerful appeal for a huge public that had been hitherto ignored, its tastes unplumbed, its buying power unsuspected — the American boy. There they were with nickels and dimes in their pockets, the lads who had just learned to read but still believed in fairy tales. Along came Alger with his story about the sixteen-year-old poor boy, sole support of his widowed mother, who begins in a menial job at four dollars a week, is fired when framed by a jealous relative, earns the friendship of a wealthy merchant and winds up well on his way to riches and the presidency of the firm. It was exactly what the youngsters wanted — a classic case of the law of supply and demand in flawless operation.

It was easy to identify with an Alger boy. Unlike Jack Harkaway or a *Chums* hero, an Alger boy never found himself imprisoned in a pit of pythons. His troubles were exceptionally real to us because they were, nine times out of ten, strictly financial. As Herbert Mayes pointed out years later, a devout disciple of the Collected Works always knew how much money an Alger boy had accumulated at any given time. If he went into a restaurant for a nourishing meal of beef stew and apple pie it was always noted that when he paid the fifteen-cent check his capital was thereby reduced to $3.47. When he got a job, his weekly expenditures of $2.85 for board and lodging, laundry, horsecar fare and church collection were subtracted from his wage of $4.00, and his consequent savings bank deposit of thirty-five cents was lovingly recorded. If he was rewarded for exposing a confidence man or an embezzler, the sum was always in cash and duly set down in his little bankbook.

In a day when few of us ever received allowances and one's spending money came by way of demolishing woodpiles or shoveling snow off walks, the financial adventures of an Alger hero were not only engrossing but easy to understand. When he got into trouble he faced the loss of his job and his life savings.

All Jack Harkaway ever risked was his neck. An Alger hero risked cash money. This peril was closer to our own experience.

But not only did Alger write the rags-to-riches story; he *was* the rags-to-riches story. He didn't create the legend. It was there all the time, waiting to be put into words. The country was full of boys anxious to believe that they too could drop out of school and become wealthy and successful. All you had to do was make the right connections, be polite to the boss, save your money and you were home free in a country where anything was possible. Alger himself proved it.

His name, in fact, has passed into the language. Whenever a tycoon dies and it emerges that he didn't make it out of Grade Ten, the obituarists have a field day describing his career as a typical Alger story and the subject as a typical Alger hero.

Now something of a minor legend, Alger has naturally attracted the attention of writers who go to a good deal of trouble trying to explain him. There isn't much to explain. He came along with the right story for the right audience at the right time, that's all.

Some philosophers have even promulgated theories that he actually exerted a profound influence on American history. Whether this influence was good or bad depends on the point of view. One school of thought (benign) contends that if it hadn't been for Alger millions of lads might have grown up indifferent to worldly success and deplorably ignorant of the necessity of getting ahead. The consequences, of course, one does not dare contemplate. The other school (malign) holds that Alger is personally to blame for the materialism that has infected American life over the past century and changed us from a people bathed in homely virtues to a murderous, lecherous rabble steeped in sin.

On another level, hardly a year goes by but some essayist dips his pen in nostalgia and recalls with affection the magic hours spent with Tom the Bootblack, Phil the Fiddler and other Alger stalwarts out back in the barn on rainy afternoons many years ago.

The tributes, however, become fewer as the years go by. Maybe he was a naive little guy, but the evidence doesn't support the suggestions of some writers that he was dim-witted. He was intelligent enough to graduate from Harvard, he was competent enough to hold down responsible jobs, he was highly regarded as a teacher and tutor. He managed his writing career with industry and acumen. Maybe he was an unfrocked pastor who preferred to chase fire engines instead of women, but in view of his parsonage background perhaps one can have sympathy for the distress he probably suffered in a society intolerant of any deviation from the hearty he-man mystique with its manly stench of beer, cigars and honest sweat. Maybe he seemed to be a prolific hack, but he refused to let himself be cheated by publishers. Several of his books called attention to social abuses of the day, especially the cruel conditions governing employment of children, and helped correct them. Maybe his heroes were insufferably smug, but they didn't steal, tell lies or throw rocks at the cops. These were negative virtues, no doubt, but better than positive evils.

He wanted to be an author, he thought of himself as an author, and he did the best he could with what he had. Which is what most of us do.

I can't read him now, but years ago he gave me hours of pleasure. More than that — a liking for books. I paid my dime. Do I owe him anything? Yes, indeed I do.

CHAPTER 16:

Sheet Anchor to Windward

I furnished my new office in Haileybury with a desk and chair bought from a politician who had just closed his campaign quarters after a disastrous election. He was glad to retrieve ten dollars from the wreckage. The desk is still in use, which works out at about twenty-one cents a year and more millions of words than anyone would believe. It was time to get going on the final book of the Hardy Boys trilogy, Volume Three, *The Secret of the Old Mill*.

Again, an old building was to be the site of strange goings-on. This one was an abandoned flour mill on the outskirts of Bayport.

I had a feeling that if the series went on for many more volumes Bayport would soon be a disaster area and our lads would qualify as authorities on crumbling architecture.

The abandoned flour mill was about as abandoned as the Old Polucca Place: the ramshackle edifice sheltered a gang of counterfeiters. It didn't have to be spelled out to the young reader that counterfeiters were very Bad Guys indeed. Young readers knew that if you couldn't depend on a five-dollar bill you couldn't depend on anything, and all commerce would crumble. As for smuggling, if the kids didn't know exactly *why* smuggling was wrong, it was enough that the United States government said it was. When the Hardy boys rounded up that gang of smugglers in Volume Two, obviously they performed a great public service. You had the Excise Department's word for it.

I was learning about villains. By and large, the villains who showed up in the abandoned buildings of Bayport were a fairly decorous bunch, a little choosy about their line of work. They didn't go in for the crude and impolite sort of thing, such as murder. Their skullduggery was on a much higher plane, involving crimes against property. Any normal lad knew that smuggling and counterfeiting were really serious offences because they struck at the very foundations of society.

The book began when the Hardy boys, on their way to the store to buy pie plates for their mother, were stopped by a stranger who needed change for a five-dollar bill. Always willing to lend a helping hand, they obliged, only to find out at the store that the bill was not legal tender. Then Fenton Hardy told them that, by an odd coincidence, he had been asked by the government to do something about a wave of counterfeit money sweeping the country.

Next, Callie Shaw's aunt, who ran a beauty shop, got hit for fifty dollars. To top it all, even Laura Hardy was taken when she sold a valuable rug for $800, every dollar of it bogus. This is probably the only time Laura was ever allowed to get in on any of the action.

Naturally the lads went after the counterfeiters with considerable zeal. With a little help from Fenton Hardy and their chums, they found a counterfeiting plant in the old mill, and went on to round up the ring of evil men who threatened the financial stability of the United States. A grateful government gave them their usual one thousand dollars by way of reward. Fenton Hardy's contribution was not recognized, but there was no need. One could assume that he clobbered the Treasury with a staggering fee.

None of this was achieved easily. The malefactors of the Old Mill were not clapped in handcuffs until Frank and Joe survived their quota of misadventures. These setbacks were invariably bloodless. A pattern had been established. No matter how ruthless and antisocial the criminals in a Hardy Boys book, nobody was ever shot, stabbed, blown up or bludgeoned to death. The Hardy boys could face extinction by fire or water, they could tumble through trapdoors and they could be pushed off cliffs, they could be captured, tied up, imprisoned and knocked on the head. But blood never flowed. We had our own code of nonviolence long before television.

Profanity, it went without saying, was a no-no. A Hardy boy or a Hardy chum might cut loose with a "gosh" or even "golly" under extreme provocation, but that was as far as he went. Even the villains, when duly captured—and they were *always* duly captured—never cursed their lot. Not even a d...n or a h...l, such as one might find in the racier adult novels of the day. Usually, they just grumbled that they would have escaped scot-free if it hadn't been for "those confounded Hardy boys," which was mighty strong talk one had to admit.

As for booze and tobacco, if a Hardy Boys' villain ever took a snort or broke open a pack of fags he did it on the sly between chapters. This probably created no end of puzzlement for young readers who attended movies, where the bad guys always did their plotting in smoke-filled dives and drank rot-gut straight, using the empty bottle to smash someone over the head, and where even the good guys rolled their own and bellied up to the bar like everyone else. Literature these books were not but, by God, they were Moral! You could fault them on any grounds you liked, but never on turpitude!

For the interest of students, it should be recorded that *The Secret of the Old Mill* introduced the stout, seaworthy craft that was to go roaring through so many subsequent volumes—the lads' own motorboat, the *Sleuth*. No longer would they be restricted to adventures on land areas accessible only to motor-cycles. The whole Atlantic Ocean was at their disposal.

They bought the *Sleuth* with their own money. After all, those thousand-dollar rewards were piling up. Fenton Hardy, stern parent that he was, handed down an edict that they could not dip into their bank account to buy gas, but they seemed to manage. They never appeared to be inhibited by lack of funds when the situation called for chasing some scalawag all over

Barmet Bay. If I had thought of it, they could have invented the credit card.

The book had another novelty. The Hardy boys, hitherto existing only on weekends, were actually seen at school. The outline didn't call for this departure, but just for the hell of it I tossed in an episode about the lads hitting the books and undergoing the torments of cramming for exams. It seemed about time.

When the script was packed off to East Orange it was duly acknowledged and a check was sent out, but Stratemeyer made no comment on my startling burst of originality. That was when I realized that these outlines weren't any more sacrosanct than the Dave Fearless specifications.

However, since Stratemeyer was obviously awaiting the verdict on the three breeders, there was no outline for Volume Four. Temporarily unemployed, I had time for some diligent work on the story about the couple trapped in the root-house and a few tales with overtones of Joseph Conrad. Unfortunately, the overtones suggested the great Mr. Korzeniowski at his turgid worst instead of at his magic best. But by this time I had acquired a New York agent who specialized in popular magazine fiction, and he returned these efforts with the comment that even original Conrads were a tough sell in the magazine field and that perhaps I had better find another model. Better still, maybe it would be just as well if I didn't imitate anybody and just let 'er rip.

I took his advice and immediately began selling. Even the root-house story found favor with *Maclean's,* Canada's biggest magazine, which was about to launch a national short story contest. The editor said he would buy this somber piece for a modest sum, if I insisted, but suggested that I enter it in the contest instead and have a shot at the first prize of $1,000. It was just the sort of thing, he thought, that might appeal to contest judges. What he meant was that it had a Canadian setting, was depressing in tone, studded with strong language and ended bleakly and without hope. I told him I would go for the big money and the concomitant fame.

Next came a package through Customs — three books, published simultaneously by Grosset and Dunlap of New York, in hard covers, bound in red, each with its frontispiece illustration by one Walter S. Rogers, who couldn't draw worth a damn. The art work in *The Tower Treasure* depicted Frank and Joe being introduced to Adelia Applegate by her brother Hurd, the stamp collector. Mr. Applegate was a weedy gent with a string tie and a vacant look. Miss Applegate, standing in a curtained archway with a flight of stairs in the background, was wearing elaborately flowing robes that seemed to have come right out of Godey's *Ladies Book* and the Hardy boys were clutching their caps in a nervous sort of way. On the whole the scene appeared to represent an elderly pimp making a pitch on behalf of a couple of youthful clients to the madam of a fashionable whorehouse. Although it was, no doubt, an interesting illustration, I thought Mr. Rogers hadn't read the book.

On the next page, in a box under the heading by Franklin W. Dixon, the three breeder titles were listed in order. A bracketed line underneath noted in small type that other volumes were in preparation. All three volumes were identical in format, with illustrations equally lacking in talent. At the back were several pages of advertisments for other publications of Grosset and Dunlap. Each page was devoted to an entire series and each series had its long list of titles.

There was the "Don Sturdy Series" by Victor Appleton, in which "Don Sturdy travels far and wide in company with his uncles, one a mighty hunter and the other a noted scientist, gaining much useful knowledge and meeting many thrilling adventures." According to the title blurbs, in one volume Don Sturdy encountered wild animals and crafty Arabs in the Sahara Desert. In another he went seeking the biggest snakes in South America and brought them back alive. (This line was pinched shamelessly from the title of a book by Frank Buck, a popular anthropologist of the day.) In still another volume young Sturdy was carried over a mighty waterfall in "the heart of gorilla land."

Clearly the hero was a landbound Dave Fearless in hard covers.

Victor Appleton, who appeared to be an inordinately pro-lific gent, was also credited with a formidable row of titles in the immortal "Tom Swift Series." Then came the "Radio Boys Series" by one Allen Chapman, who also authored the "Rail-road Boys Series." If you were a train buff or a kid with his first crystal set, Allen Chapman was your man. If Westerns were your dish, however, Grosset and Dunlap had some good ones for you in "The X-Bar-X Boys," featuring Roy and Teddy Manley, "sons of an old ranchman, owner of many thousands of head of cattle, lads who know how to ride, how to shoot and how to take care of themselves under all circumstances whether *In Thunder Canyon*, *On Whirlpool River* or *On Big Bison Trail*."

The creator of "The X-Bar-X Boys" was identified as James Cody Ferris, himself a bona fide Old Westerner and a veteran of the range. I would have been considerably astonished had I known that one day I would step into the high-heeled boots of James Cody Ferris—for one volume only—when that grizzled plainsman was apparently laid low by a rattlesnake bite or a kick from some ornery cayuse. In spite of first-hand knowledge that Edward Stratemeyer managed a whole stable of writers, I was still so innocent that the Grosset and Dunlap imprint fooled me. I thought the volumes advertised at the back of the book were Grosset and Dunlap books not necessarily from the Stratemeyer production line.

Innocent? I was just plain *dumb*! I really believed in Victor Appleton, Allen Chapman and James Cody Ferris, although I had just unwrapped three books by Franklin W. Dixon, whom I knew didn't exist because he was me. Believe it or not, I didn't realize that *all* the advertised books came from the Stratemeyer fiction factory and that, indeed, they represented merely a small part of a prodigious output.

However, there lay the three books, my first hardcovers, in highly visible crimson binding, good readable type, more than 200 pages each, copyrighted in the Library of Congress, looking a good deal more imposing and far more durable than any of the Dave Fearless characters.

I think they sold for seventy-five cents. I am uncertain

about this because I never bought one. It was a long time before a Hardy Boys book reached Haileybury, perhaps because they were banned by the local library as deleterious to young minds. On my occasional visits to Toronto it never occurred to me to look for them in real bookstores.

Now they were launched on the sea of juvenile opinion. Would they be greeted with apathy, politely tolerated or rejected with scorn? On the other hand, would they be received with enthusiasm, read with joy, applauded by boyish huzzahs? This may have been of concern to Edward Stratemeyer, Alex Grosset and George Dunlap. It was of absolutely no concern to me. I was merely a ghost. Does a wraith have anxieties? Does a spook fret about sales? No one could have cared less.

I gathered that the breeders must have done reasonably well in the marketplace when Stratemeyer sent along another outline called *The Missing Chums*. Who was missing? Chet Morton and Biff Hooper, held for ransom by a bunch of bank robbers.

It hinged on a big mistake. The robbers thought all along that they were kidnapping the Hardy boys. When they discovered their error, it was too late to say: "Sorry, kids. We thought you was two other guys." The mistake cost them, of course, because the Hardy boys were free to spend the whole book working on the case and there could be only one outcome. The bank robbers were captured, the chums were set free and Frank and Joe snaffled another handsome reward.

With the outline, however, came a disturbing letter. It concerned my beloved Keystone Kops. Stratemeyer felt that the volumes already written suggested a grievous lack of respect for officers of the law! He regretted that I seemed to regard Messrs. Collig, Smuff and Riley as figures of fun. He did not think this was wise. The effect on growing boys must be considered. In future volumes it would be well to treat the Bayport constabulary with the respect to which they were entitled.

I couldn't believe it. There was something wrong with this

drastic change of attitude. Why, for example, had Stratemeyer bestowed the name of Smuff on that defective detective in the first place if he wanted the fellow to be held in respect? How could any lad with a scrap of intelligence stand in awe of a cop called Smuff? If the Hardy boys went around tugging their forelocks whenever they encountered Detective Smuff, all young readers would just naturally regard them as stupid. Even stupider than Smuff himself!

And why, if Stratemeyer felt so strongly about the matter, hadn't he done a little editing on the scripts? The cops were already on the printed record as bumbling imbeciles. Five minutes with a blue pencil could have sanctified them, made them grave enforcers of the law, devoted to their trade. Definitely, something had happened when the books went on sale. Maybe Franklin K. Mathiews had pounced again.

I groaned. There went my best source of comedy material. I had been counting on the Bayport Bluecoats for at least four chapters of surefire laughs per book, and if I had any strong conviction about the Hardy Boys Series at all, it was that where kid readers were concerned you couldn't go wrong by larding the action with a little funny stuff. However, when a sheet of paper went into the machine for the opening page of *The House on the Cliff*, I realized glumly that Collig & Co. would have to shape up and the Hardy boys would have to be polite to the cops if it killed them.

But I had my own thoughts about teaching youngsters that obedience to authority is somehow sacred. Where did it say that kids shouldn't size up people for themselves? Was it written in the Bible, the Talmud, the Koran, the British North America Act and the Constitution of the United States that everyone in authority was inflexibly honest, pious and automatically admirable? Would civilization crumble if kids got the notion that the people who ran the world were sometimes stupid, occasionally wrong and even corrupt at times? Was it a favor to let them grow up dumbly assuming that all is for the best in the best of all possible worlds? Wouldn't every kid be the better for a little shot of healthy skepticism at an early age?

Of course. And a lot of good that philosophy did me. Chief Collig suddenly became the sagacious head of an efficient police department. Detective Smuff miraculously acquired wisdom in spite of his name. Constable Riley was strangely transformed into a lovable cop on the beat and a friend to all.

Unexpectedly, however, just as I was choking on these mandatory developments, a ray of sunshine appeared. It had become clear to Stratemeyer, just as it had long been obvious to me, that Laura Hardy was a very pallid character. The outlines practically ignored the good woman and, for the life of me, I couldn't find very much for her to do. She seemed to spend most of her time making sandwiches to go. She served as an admiring listener whenever the men of the family came home long enough to discuss their exploits of crime-busting in the great world, but this function as sounding board was pretty limited.

And now, of all things, Stratemeyer decided that she needed help. Because Fenton Hardy and sons were scheduled to be away from home for long stretches of Volume Four, he suggested that a maiden aunt should come a-visiting to keep Mrs. Hardy company.

Gold! Pure, gleaming, high-grade gold!

I doubt if Stratemeyer intended her to be amusing. If he did, he may have considered that if I insisted on being funny the ribaldry had better be kept in the family rather than directed at the Bayport Police Force. If I couldn't contain myself in the presence of Detective Smuff maybe a domestic lightning rod might help. If that was his thinking, it worked. I looked on the visiting relative as a godsend, spat on my hands and joyfully went to work making Aunt Gertrude a Character.

She arrived in Bayport on the afternoon train one day toward the end of Chapter Six, complete with handbags, parcels, a mountain of luggage and a yellow cat named Lavinia. She climbed out of a cab in front of the Hardy home, bawled out the driver in a dispute over the fare, bellowed for the Hardy boys to come carry her luggage and then gave them hell because they didn't hustle. She went right on giving them hell during every scene in which she appeared for the rest of the book, and I saw to it that she had more scenes than kindly, sandwich-spreading Laura Hardy had achieved in all the previous books or the series put together. She certainly livened up an otherwise routine narrative and more than compensated for the transmutations of Collig and Company.

If there was a turning point in the series this was it. Maybe a turning point wasn't needed. Maybe the series would have plodded along without her but it wouldn't have been the same. Whether the Hardy Boys sales zoomed upward after the arrival of Aunt Gertrude in Volume Four, I can't say for sure but it is highly probable, because after that volume Stratemeyer gave instructions that Aunt Gertrude was to be a permanent member of the cast.

He never actually came right out and complimented me on Aunt Gertrude. You could always count on him to keep his head and steel himself against giving writers fancy notions about their importance. It was enough that the lady appeared in every outline thereafter.

For a while she merely showed up from time to time on visits. After a time she settled in as a member of the household where she asserted herself so formidably that Laura Hardy receded farther into the background.

Kid readers who had merely tolerated Laura Hardy just loved Aunt Gertrude. They knew there was a heart of gold under that crusty exterior. When she bawled out the Hardy boys, which she did continually, she was actually telling them she loved them. Had she come right out and said so, the while smothering them with big, fat, slobbery kisses, young readers would have been disgusted. As it was, she made them feel that here was one who really cared.

In fact, in the late Thirties, when there was a project to launch a Hardy Boys radio program based on the books, it was to have been called "Aunt Gertrude and the Boys." The old termagant had pushed the kids right out of stage center. The death of Edna Mae Oliver, who was to have been the star, terminated the project. It was inconceivable that anyone else could have played Aunt Gertrude. Even in recent years, when the Hardy boys made it in television as cartoon characters in primary colors with their own rock theme blaring away and two completely altered plots jammed into one program (a ridiculous show that polluted the morning air for nearly a year), Laura Hardy was not among the characters but Aunt Gertrude survived.

A school teacher told me a while back that when she asked her class to name their favorite characters in fiction she found Aunt Gertrude right up there with Huckleberry Finn. This caused her no little embarrassment. She had never heard of Aunt Gertrude and didn't care to lose face by asking. Obviously she had been living far outside the mainstream of juvenile culture. She had to sidle off and make inquiries of the principal. He enlightened her but gave her a very strange look. "As if he thought maybe I was too dumb to be teaching English," she said.

By the time I had finished *The Missing Chums*, another outline had arrived: *Hunting for Hidden Gold*. The lads were packed off to the Far West, where they ended up in the usual ruined structure, of course — this time an abandoned mine.

Without realizing it I had acquired systematic work habits and a professional attitude. The morning chapter rolled out of the typewriter every day until the book was done, the order filled, the merchandise delivered. Of the material written during the other working hours, fewer stories came back. The gloomy tale about the settler and his family didn't win the big prize in the all-Canadian short story contest, but it shared third. That was no great honor but it earned a good deal of publicity and an anthologist asked leave to put it in his book. Canadian magazines actually requested material. Bob Hardy, my New York agent, found editors who sent checks.

The professional attitude was difficult to define. If one is willing to accept money for writing a certain kind of material, he should do his best. The young, the uncultured or unsophisticated reader is not to blame for his condition and should not be despised — certainly not by the writer who lives by that reader's nickels and dimes.

The Dave Fearless outlines had been outrageous fantasies, bordering on burlesque. Viewed in one light, they were comic works. "The Hardy Boys" were likewise contrived for wish fulfillment but I had learned not to despise them. They had their lowly place in the world of commercial publishing, with its variety of reading matter as infinite as the mind of man. They were written swiftly, but not carelessly. I gave thought to grammar, sentence structure, choice of words, pace, the techniques of suspense, all within the limits of the medium which was in this case mass-produced, assembly-line fiction for boys. Every kind of writing, from the ancient morality plays to a modern television series, has its own boundaries, and the writer who seeks to earn a living learns the boundaries and works within them. As for the writer of talent, or even genius, perhaps it is better for him and for the world that he earn bread and shelter in any other way than by the sale of words.

I knew I was not a genius and moreover that genius cannot be achieved by effort. I also knew that I was not a writer of great talent, although even a small talent can be improved and developed by diligence. I probably had a knack for story telling, the entertainer's gift which can always be polished to the glow of art. One should be thankful for any gift, however small. I enjoyed using it and there was double enjoyment in the thought that it might give some pleasure to others. One had to guard against self-deception, in mistaking the gift for talent which was somehow deserving of esteem. Honesty was everything. There could be some excuse for poor work but never for dishonest work. Lack of talent might be regrettable but it is not, after all, a mortal sin. The obligation was to do one's best with the gifts one had.

As time passed, more and more stories found their way into magazines in Canada, in the United States, even in England, and some of them were very good magazines indeed. Not the magazines of high circulation, which paid handsomely and where the competiton was comparably keen and dominated by veteran writers, but magazines in which one was not ashamed to appear. I began to entertain heady notions about getting out of the Hardy Boys business.

There were other heady notions as well. Ideas about marriage. Fred Wallace, a Scottish sailor turned author, once advised me that no one should ever launch his craft as a full-time writer without dropping "a sheet anchor to windward." He cautioned that this applied most particularly to any writer who had taken unto himself a wife. In other words, some reliable source of income, however small, was necessary.

So, I wrote to Stratemeyer and asked him how the Hardy Boys books were doing and how strongly I could depend on them as a source of secondary income. I suggested that the payment was small. An increase seemed in order. Actually I was interested in the sales of the books merely to the extent that they might indicate that I was worth more money.

Mr. Stratemeyer replied that he hoped to publish two Hardy Boys books a year and that he hoped he could count on me to supply them. That was all. He didn't mention money. He didn't mention sales figures. I learned later that Edward Stratemeyer was not a man who ever confided sales figures to his score of ghosts. It wasn't because he was afraid this kind of information would encourage the spooks to ask for more money if a series found favor. He had ways of dealing with that. He simply felt it was none of their business.

A request for a raise wouldn't have done a spook any good anyway. When Stratemeyer struck a price that price was final. A spook could be replaced with alarming ease. Stratemeyer didn't come right out and say so, but one had a mental picture of a block-long lineup of eager candidates waiting outside his office to pinch-hit for any rebellious Oliver Twist rash enough to ask for more.

Nor would it have helped to seek out a companion spook and compare notes. They were anonymous, invisible, unidentifiable, impossible to find. I met one of them quite by accident years later and he said Stratemeyer conferred with writers only by appointment and that he took good care to see that appointments were judiciously spaced. No two spooks ever found themselves waiting side by side on the bench and in a position to compare notes or even to discover that each was Roy Rockwood or even (God forbid) Laura Lee Hope, renowned since 1906 as authoress of the Bobbsey Twins.

Gloomily, I considered Stratemeyer's reply. Optimistically, then, I told myself that it was only a matter of time before I would be making a hefty income from the magazines and even from book publishers. Until then, Stratemeyer could count on his two books a year.

And so, with a check for a Hardy Boys book in my pocket and an order for another, along with encouraging words of promise from a few editors, Amy Arnold and I were married in Montreal and went to live in a little village nearby. If our parents thought us insane they refrained from comment. We defined our action as merely indicating confidence in the future. After all, I had my sheet anchor to windward — two Frank-and-Joe books a year. Not a very strong anchor, to be sure, but better than none at all. The sheet anchor was to hold far longer than I ever planned. It held through several nasty squalls and one almighty hurricane for sixteen more volumes and a few other books I would just as soon forget. Nearly fifteen years went by before the rope was cut. It was considerably frayed by that time anyway.

CHAPTER 17:

The Last of the Hardy Boys

When my young wife told her friends that she had married a writer, their good wishes sounded more like condolences. Especially a Canadian writer! One good woman said, "God help you, my dear!" with compassion. We thought it amusing at the time. Later we realized what she meant.

Writers are not good husband material. (I am not qualified to speak for the husbands of female writers.) Not because they are worse characters than men of other occupations. They aren't. Not because they are impractical and untidy. They are. Not because their income is chancy. It is. But they are always underfoot. The unbroken presence of a mate who hammers at a typewriter and bawls for silence can become, at the very least, irksome. In fact, he turns into an intolerable nuisance. Every time she lays eyes on the pest she is provoked into considering his imperfections.

When he summons her into his presence occasionally so that he may read aloud some particularly happy expression of his genius, she must applaud if she knows what is good for her. Otherwise the Master will be hurt and go into a fit of the sulks. When a story is going well, he withdraws into another world, gazes at her as if wondering who she is and where she came from, sits at the dinner table mumbling to himself. When a story goes badly, he mopes and becomes unfit for human society. The days turn on the arrival of the postman with good news or bad — or even worse, no news at all.

Who can blame her if she envies her sisters whose husbands clear out every morning and stay the hell out until dinner time, returning with fascinating accounts of their adventures in the great world, of the installation of the new water cooler and how he told off the assistant manager?

My life has been blessed by two remarkably happy marriages, each happy because of a woman who had the cheerful courage and devotion to put up with an existence calculated to drive most wives to a psychiatric hospital or divorce court. Here is where a writer has some small advantage. He can strike his own medals. So, to the memory of one now dead and the living presence of another, a paragraph of love and gratitude is little enough and not nearly enough.

The sheet anchor gave me the time needed for a horrendous novel about crime in the Montreal underworld, a region I knew only by evil repute. The book was serialized in a good magazine, found publishers in New York and London, got good reviews and earned an option for three more. A dozen good magazines began buying other stories.

But there was always time for another Hardy Boys. America was prospering and so was the Syndicate, so Stratemeyer stepped up the price to $150, later raised a little higher.

For the benefit of the buffs, perhaps it is time to recapitulate.

The buff is a male phenomenon; there are few female buffs. Sometimes he is a child, more often he is a grown man, aging a little and inclined to look back on happier days. They collect, and even read again, literature that once gave them pleasure. There are buffs who haunt dusty, old stores looking for ancient movie magazines. Some seek old comic books and prize early copies of Superman. There are Alger buffs and Tarzan buffs, Tom Swift buffs and Rover Boys buffs. By trade and purchase they accumulate collections. They write letters, frequently to writers untraceable or even dead. They are not to be confused with fans, who are usually very young and merely scrawl letters expressing admiration.

The buff wants details. How and when was a book written? What was the date of publication? He recalls characters and incidents which found favor with him. He tells you about the volumes he has on his shelves and how they were acquired. He is a True Believer. He is the mainstay of Ye Olde Booke Mart in all its strange manifestations. Now that my cover has been blown, he writes to me all the time.

The Shore Road Mystery was published in 1928 (following *Hunting for Hidden Gold*, published in the same year). It began with the theft of Isa Fussy's brand-new $2,800 Cadillac, which was a fancy price for the time. The Hardy boys became involved when one of their chums was arrested for the crime. After bailing him out they felt it incumbent upon them to solve the mystery because other cars also disappeared. They hit upon the ingenious scheme of buying an old car as bait and hiding in the trunk. By way of comic relief there was an excruciating chapter on one of Chet's practical jokes when he bought a dead fish and planted it in Frank Hardy's desk at school. Imagine Chet's discomfiture when Frank discovered the fish and planted it in Chet's desk and the teacher found it. Rib-tickling stuff. Anyhow, after various adventures in the caves of Barmet Bay, the lads tracked down the gang of automobile thieves and the police rounded them up. The Automobile Club of Bayport came through with a reward of $1,500. The money was presented, of course, at a banquet in honor of Frank and Joe. It was remiss of me but I neglected to go into detail about the menu, which probably disappointed many readers. Hurd Applegate, his sister Adelia and the Robinsons, late of *The Tower Treasure* popped up long enough to comment admiringly. Mr. Applegate, the stamp collector, said that if he had his say he would print a special stamp in their honor. Adelia said the boys were "as brave as the knights of old." But Tessie Robinson said Frank and Joe Hardy ought to be in a book.

The Secret of the Caves is imprinted on my memory for the

reason that it represented a feat of very swift writing. I ran out of money in Toronto and needed a check in a hurry. Joe Mac-Dougall, a friend who edited a humorous magazine called *Goblin*, had a couple of vacant offices because his magazine, to which I contributed once in a while, had fallen on hard times. Joe loaned me an office and a typewriter.

I rattled off a fast 50,000 words that began when the Hardy boys rescued Evangeline Todd from a burning boat when she was on her way to Bayport to consult Fenton Hardy about her missing brother, Todham Todd, who had mislaid his memory. There were strange doings in the Honeycomb Caves — whenever things got dull the Hardy boys headed straight for a cave if they couldn't find an abandoned house. They encountered a daft sailor called Captain Royal, who fell off a cliff and was rescued by the boys. Naturally he turned out to be Todham Todd. This time the boys refused a reward but they got the mandatory banquet with roast chicken and ice cream. I wrote the book in five days, delayed because McDougall kept bringing friends around to watch.

The Mystery of Cabin Island began when the boys were iceboating on Barmet Bay and were ordered off mysterious Cabin Island by a couple of rascals named Ike Nash and Tad Carson, who also wrecked their boat. This was a complicated tale in which the boys earned the friendship of antique dealer Jefferson, owner of Cabin Island, who gave them permission to use his cabin any time they wished. A storekeeper told the boys how Jefferson had married Mary Bender, who had inherited a valuable stamp collection which was apparently stolen by a servant named John Sparewell. The boys found a notebook with Sparewell's name, a cipher message and a map of Cabin Island. They went to the cabin, were trapped by a storm, a fallen tree wrecked the chimney and Frank found the box which held the stamp collection (hidden in the fireplace when the cabin was built). The stamps were returned to collector Jefferson who came across with a measly $100 reward and no banquet, the cheapie!

The Great Airport Mystery brought the Hardy boys into the

air age, when a drunken pilot crashed his plane and nearly killed them in their roadster while driving near the new airport. Then the boys overheard the pilot, Giles Ducroy, conferring with some shady characters in a shack near the airport. On an outing to Cabin Island they learned of a $20,000 mail robbery at the airport. Much to their astonishment the Hardy boys were arrested for the robbery, but they discovered that good deeds are always rewarded when Hurd Applegate and antique collector Jefferson, from previous volumes, came up with the bail money of $50,000. (Obviously, those previous volumes came in handy.) Finally, in a truly breathtaking display of ignorance of aircraft, the boys stowed away on Giles Ducroy's plane and broke up an attempt to hijack a mail plane.

The Great Aircraft Mystery was written left-handed while I was finishing another novel, turning out half a dozen stories for magazines and prospering. I decided that it was time to haul in the sheet anchor to windward. Who needed the Hardy boys when everything was going so well?

The outline of *What Happened at Midnight* had just arrived. I debated sending it back. However, I decided that I couldn't let Stratemeyer down, so I whacked into an opening scene in the Bayport automat wherein the lads had a friendly scuffle with boys from Crabb's Corners and went on to a party at Chet Morton's farm. When Iola and Joe invited the Crabb's Corners boys, in the goodness of their hearts, to join the party for ice cream, Joe was dragged into the bushes and disappeared for days. Aunt Gertrude arrived for one of her memorable visits to the Hardy home and told of a fair-haired man who was rude to her on the train.

The boys did a lot of traveling in this one. Frank went looking for Joe in the motorboat and found him — where else? — in a cave. They saw Aunt Gertrude's fair-haired man but lost him when he bought a ticket to New York. The Hardy boys followed, tracked him to an import office, then to a restaurant. In a hotel they overheard a man phoning the Bayport YMCA but before they could do anything about it Frank's wallet was lifted. They began hitchhiking back to Bayport, were picked up by two strangers who turned out to be Department of Justice operatives hot on the trail of a big smuggling ring. Back in Bayport, Aunt Gertrude told them her fair-haired man was working in a local drug store, but when they tried to run him down he took off in a plane. They followed and after a dangerous parachute jump they rounded up the smugglers and collected a reward of $2,000.

That did it. I made up my mind to turn down the next outline, say farewell to Frank and Joe forever and relinquish my shroud to some other ghost. My wife and I made plans for the future. We decided to move to Bermuda, which had not yet been taken over by the tourist industry and where two — by now three — could live handsomely on American dollars.

So much for mice and men. We never did get to Bermuda. And I was grateful to accept the next assignment, *While the Clock Ticked*, and to go right on churning out Hardy Boys books for Stratemeyer.

The answer is in the date: October, 1929.

Men who have been through a war seldom care to talk about their experiences to those who haven't. There is a feeling that only those who have shared the grubby reality can understand it. It was that way about the Great Depression, almost invariably capitalized, like the Great Plague. Stories of death and danger can be absorbing, but stories of debt and poverty are always infinitely tiresome. Reminiscences of the Depression are not in favor.

When commerce collapsed, advertising collapsed with it. Magazine chains retrenched or foundered. Publishing houses went under. Editors stopped buying and used up the unpublished scripts that jammed the office safes, if they survived at all. Established authors borrowed against royalties that never came, cashed in their bonds, sold their homes. Their freelance brothers faced destitution. One could not, literally, give stories away. Joe Rutledge, an editor who had become a dear friend, returned a better-than-usual story with a letter saying that the amount his magazine, *The Canadian*, could afford was so small that he was ashamed to offer it. He begged me to hold "Alias Mr. Pollard" until conditions improved and then send it to some editor who could pay what it was worth. Conditions didn't improve. After two years I sent it back to him. He scraped up fifty dollars and mailed it with apologies. Subsequently, over the years, it earned more than a hundred times that sum in radio, television and anthology rights.

There was so much that was demeaning about the Depression, such wreckage of hopes, plans, careers and human pride, that few survivors care to look back on those years. There was no unemployment insurance, no ready resort to authorities for a weekly or monthly check under the euphemism of social welfare. If a family became penniless, there was merely "relief" in dibs and dabs of food and fuel, grudgingly dispensed by a municipality that couldn't collect its taxes. And there was an old stigma attached to these bounties, the stigma of failure. Proud people would starve before they would let their plight become known. The women bore the worst of it. Always there was the effort to shield the children from the knowledge of desperation.

There was one bad week when I had two short story manuscripts ready and couldn't scrape up enough pennies for the postage. It would have been easier to ask a friend for the loan of a hundred dollars than seventy-eight cents. The pennies wouldn't have helped anyway. Story markets were dead.

Although some series were cut from the list during the Depression, and even more were dropped during World War II, the Hardy Boys held firm along with the immortal Bobbsey Twins and Nancy Drew. Somehow the kids—or their relatives —dug up the necessary nickels and dimes so that the little addicts could have their fix.

There was no longer any thought of abandoning the sheet anchor to windward; for a while we subsisted almost entirely on the few orders that came from the Syndicate, although the price had been cut and the Canadian dollar was at an awesome discount. On one memorable occasion the check amounted to a mere $85.00 Canadian. What was worse, Roosevelt declared his bank holiday on the day the check arrived, so it couldn't even be cashed.

These pittances were manifestly better than no money at all. And there was something else—a mere straw: the Syndicate would make an advance, and one advance only, on future work. All writers know about the advance. However welcome at the time, it is an ancient trap. The advance is always spent before the work is finished, so another advance becomes necessary. This is the principle behind a form of bondage which may not have been invented by the canny Mr. Hensloe in Elizabethan times, but which he found very useful, as revealed when he remarked of certain impecunious playwrights: "Should these fellowes come out of my debt I should have noe rule over them."

Mr. Hensloe needed plays for the company which performed in his theater and, because playwriting was a new art, there weren't many playwrights around. Those who were available were usually unreliable tosspots, prone to promising scripts and getting drunk after delivering the first act, especially if they had been paid for the entire play. So Mr. Hensloe doled out money judiciously. One of the better playwrights, fellow by the name of Shakespeare, escaped the trap because he became a shareholder in another theater, The Globe, but other scribblers were not so lucky.

I was one fellowe who had noe success at all in coming out of debt, and so I went on as Franklin W. Dixon far longer than I ever intended.

One day in 1930 a letter from the Syndicate advised that Edward Stratemeyer had died of pneumonia at the age of sixty-eight. His age matched the number of pen names he had used during his life, including forty-seven which had been Stratemeyer Syndicate house names. There were such names among them as E. Ward Strayer, Jim Bowie, Ned St. Myer, Dr. Willard Mackenzie, May Hollis Barton, Laura Lee Hope, Amy Bell Marlow, Carolyn Keene and even Lester Chadwick. One redoubtable pseudonym actually fathered itself when Victor

Appleton became Victor Appleton II. Stratemeyer's biography in *Contemporary Authors* ran to two pages of small, closely packed type, more than 3,000 words, of which 2,500 words consisted of the titles of the books with which he had been connected one way or the other. The list ran to more than three of the four columns.

I had never met him, had never even spoken to him on the telephone. At the time of my marriage, he sent a wedding check for $25 and a similar check on the birth of our first daughter. Now the letter said that in his will he bequeathed each of his writers a sum equal to one-fifth of their earnings from the Syndicate. Although he was all business when it came to dealings that involved the Syndicate, he had his kind side. I had a feeling of loss.

It was announced that his daughters, Mrs. Harriet Adams and Miss Edna Stratemeyer, would carry on the work of the Syndicate from the old office in the Hall Building in East Orange, N.J. Mrs. Harriet Adams, who wrote under the name of Carolyn Keene, was already world famed as the creator of Nancy Drew, a girl detective who eclipsed even *Bomba the Jungle Boy* in sales figures, and cashed in on a vast public that had been neglected since the days of the immortal Elsie Dinsmore.

Nancy Drew and the Hardy Boys were doing so well that the Syndicate decided to launch a new series which would combine the best features of both. The Hardy Boys had shown that two heroes were better than one, because they always had someone to talk to and they could take turns in being rescuer and rescuee. So why not *two* Nancy Drews?

Hence, The Dana Girls, a sort of distaff Hardy Boys venture about a pair of sisters named Jean and Louise Dana. To avoid bothersome family complications, they attended Starhurst Boarding School but, like Nancy, Frank and Joe, they solved innocuous mysteries between classes.

Mrs. Adams (now the Syndicate) asked me to do three breeders, beginning with a title called *In the Shadow of the Tower*. It was 1934 and things were tough. I felt almighty foolish about becoming Carolyn Keene, but my wife promised she wouldn't tell anyone. So I spent a couple of months banging away at the Dana sisters. Perhaps the expression is indelicate. Nobody ever banged the Dana girls — at least not for the record. Occasionally, I was tempted to turn them loose in one of Bayport's numerous abandoned buildings with the Hardy boys, just to see what would happen. It might have done the whole four of them no end of good.

After the breeders were launched I did another volume. Then the whole thing became too much for me and I begged off. Starvation seemed preferable. The series went on, because no ghost is irreplaceable. It is still going on, in fact, but the Dana Girls have never really threatened Nancy Drew. Maybe the breeders lacked something. Perhaps the virgins who followed the adventures of Jean and Louise sensed a lack of empathy.

I never felt comfortable as Carolyn Keene, and I was glad to don Franklin W. Dixon's cap again. For the record (and for the buffs):

A Sinister Signpost, 1936, had to do with the disappearance of a valuable racehorse and concluded when Aunt Gertrude bawled out the boys on the iniquities of the track, then received a lawyer's letter informing her that she had been bequeathed a stable of horses.

A Figure in Hiding, 1937, was a mishmash which began with the hold-up of a Bayport theater box office, the mysterious activities of a pretty girl named Virginia and a phony eye doctor who called himself Grafton. There was also a deaf-mute, a character named Zeb and an associate villain named Rip Sinder. The boys broke up the "eye syndicate," recovered the stolen money and picked up a reward of $500. After all, this was the Depression and rewards were sadly deflated.

The Secret Warning, 1938, has passed completely out of my memory and my records, definitely a loss to posterity.

We were living in the small town of Whitby, near Toronto, when the Depression was ended by the war. I spent an entire morning sitting naked in a drafty recruiting hall with a dog tag around my neck, until somebody remembered to tell me I had been rejected for service because I wasn't tall enough. It seemed odd that no one noticed that when I showed up. It was a humiliating experience, from which I gained only a head cold.

The Flickering Torch Mystery, 1943, was written in a stifling room during a heat wave in wartime Ottawa. The very thought of it brings out perspiration.

An odd thing happened while I was sweating this one out. I had broken into radio, doing a long series of plays for the Canadian Broadcasting Corporation, and ventured into history with a little piece about Sir John A. Macdonald. In the course of the play it was necessary for the future Prime Minister of Canada to spend a little time in a country blacksmith shop during repairs to his carriage. I thought it would lend authenticity if I could come up with the name of Sir John's coachman. So I spent about a week on research, reading everything I could find about Macdonald's life, but the coachman's name always eluded me. A week after the play went on the air, with the name of Macdonald's secretary substituted for that of the coachman, I was toiling at *The Flickering Torch Mystery* when I looked out the window and saw a funeral in progress at a house across the street. While the search for the coachman's identity had been going on, I had noticed an elderly man enjoying the shade of the veranda. Then he had disappeared. The next morning the *Ottawa Journal* ran a brief story about the funeral. It provided the name I had been seeking in vain. The funeral was for a man who once been coachman for Sir John A. Macdonald.

We moved to Ottawa, where I drew a regular paycheck for the first time in years doing public relations work for the Department of Munitions and Supply. About a year later John Grierson, who had come from England to establish the National Film Board of Canada, invited me to join his group of documentary film makers. They toiled in an abandoned sawmill and I thought they were all demented, with the exception of the great Grierson and a weedy disciple named Norman MacLaren.

I never could understand why I was hired because Grierson didn't think writers belonged in documentary film work and never hesitated to express his low opinion of them. You didn't write films; you directed and edited films. Grierson didn't believe in actors, either. Or sets. Documentary film was a Movement, concerned with normal people going about their normal concerns in a normal way. The trouble was that when you brought lights and cameras into a lumber camp or an aircraft factory and aimed them at anyone at work people ceased to work naturally. Give them lines to say and they forgot the words, mumbled and stumbled, and all illusion vanished.

So I became a director and spent the next fifteen years roaming from the coast of Gaspé to the lush valleys of the Caribou country in British Columbia with camera and sound crews. My wife, who had just become nicely adjusted to an underfoot husband, was now obliged to adjust to a husband who was seldom at home at all. She managed the one just as she had survived the other. The films I made are now forgotten, although I won a few awards in a field where it is difficult to escape getting awards. I wrote a script for a documentary short subject called "Herring Hunt" which was nominated for a Hollywood Oscar and didn't win, and for a feature called "Royal Journey" which was nominated for a British Film Academy Award, and did.

As for the Hardy Boys, after *The Short Wave Mystery* (in which the boys went scientific) and *The Secret Panel*, I bowed out with *The Phantom Freighter* which was written in 1946 in motel rooms at night on a location in Nova Scotia when I was directing a film. For me, that was the end of the Hardy Boys. I didn't need them any more, and certainly they didn't need me, because they have continued to this day.

There was no quarrel, no dramatic break with the Syndicate for which I had toiled over a period of twenty years and ground out more than two million words. I merely sent in the manuscript with a note to the effect that I was too busy to take on any further assignments. The Syndicate didn't plead with me to continue. In fact, the Syndicate didn't seem to care much one way or the other. Other spooks were always available. If the parting involved any emotion at all, it was one of relief, as if a couple of relatives who came for the weekend had finally moved on after sticking around for years.

I was pretty bored with the Hardy boys by that time anyway. Not with the books, because I never read them. Whenever a new one arrived I might skim through a few pages and then the volume would join its predecessors on a bookcase shelf. Under glass, like a row of embalmed owls, so the dust wouldn't get at them.

Perhaps a psychologist would have been interested in this extraordinary indifference to the physical evidence of work that had occupied so many hours over so many years (about twenty volumes in all, ending with *The Phantom Freighter*), not counting the Dave Fearless paperbacks, the Dana Girls and assorted extras that have utterly vanished from my memory. But to me it was if some force within my mind insisted on thrusting the books into limbo the moment the final page of a final chapter came out of the typewriter. Not revulsion. Complete indifference. Perhaps this also accounted for the fact that, although I had been in New York many times, I was never tempted to cross the river and drop into the Stratemeyer Syndicate office in East Orange. I had nothing whatever against Edward Stratemeyer or his daughters or the Syndicate people, and I am sure I would have been welcome, but somehow it just never seemed to matter. The dozens of stories I had written for magazines good and bad on both sides of the Atlantic were all carefully collected and bound, some of them occasionally reread, but I never curled up with a Hardy Boys book to spend a happy hour reading it all the way through.

It was not until sometime in the 1940s, as a matter of fact, that I had discovered that Franklin W. Dixon and the Hardy Boys were conjurable names. One day my son had come into the workroom, which had never been exalted into a "study," and pointed to the bookcase with its shelf of Hardy Boys originals. "Why do you keep these books, Dad? Did you read them when you were a kid?"

"Read them? I wrote them." And then, because it doesn't do to deceive any youngster, "At least, I wrote the words."

He stared. I saw incredulity. Then open-mouthed respect.

"Why didn't you tell me?"

"I suppose it never occurred to me."

This was true. The Hardy Boys were never mentioned in the household. They were never mentioned to friends. Maybe it was a holdover from Edward Stratemeyer's long past injunction to secrecy. Habit. I wasn't ashamed of them. I had done them as well as I could, at the time. They had merely provided a way of making a living.

"But they're wonderful books," he said. "I used to borrow them from the other kids all the time until I found them here."

"Other kids read them?"

"Dad, where have you been? Everybody reads them. You can buy them in Simpson's. Shelves of them."

Next day I went to the department store and damned if the lad wasn't right! They *did* have shelves of them. There were *The Tower Treasure*, *The House on the Cliff*, *The Secret of the Old Mill*, *The Great Airport Mystery*, all the remembered titles, the whole score of them, and more I had never heard of. And over on another shelf, a dozen titles in the Dana Girls series, considerably outnumbered by a massive collection of Nancy Drew.

I began to see the Hardy Boys books wherever I went, in small bookstores and large, even in railway depots and corner stores. There seemed to be an epidemic. Whenever I saw a small boy on a train or plane, he was almost invariably absorbed in a bright blue volume, lost in Bayport and environs. "They must have sold a lot of those things," I reflected. "Maybe a hundred thousand or so."

I asked a clerk if the Hardy Boys books were popular.

"Most popular boys' books we carry," he said. "Matter of fact, they're supposed to be the best-selling boys' books in the world."

"Imagine that!" I said in downright wonderment.

CHAPTER 18:

The Dispossessed Ghost

The Film Board experience ended with the death of my wife in 1955. She had lived to make her husband happy and to see our three children grown, graduated and married. I left Ottawa, took to writing for television, and was invited to become drama editor of the Canadian Broadcasting Corporation. I met Bea Kenney, a widow, who didn't mind having a husband underfoot, married again and went back to freelancing once more.

Perhaps I missed the freedom and the exhilarating element of risk. It's a chancy life, this business of spinning words and scenes out of your head — literally living by your wits. A survival course. The magazines offered a living for a while, the magazines gave way to radio, which in turn gave way to television, and if you couldn't adapt to the market you perished. But in the beginning was the word, and as long as there are people to read them there will be people to buy them.

The other day someone asked my friend, MacKinlay Kantor, when he planned to retire. Our paths in life have differed vastly but we both are of the same age, began on small-town newspapers, made a living from the pulps, and are still writing. "Writers," replied Kantor, in a voice that came mighty close to a snarl, "*never* retire. Real writers, that is." And we wouldn't have it any other way. It is a survival course that never ends for any of us. I will be freelancing until someone draws the cover over my typewriter for me for the last time.

Whenever I am interviewed, which is oftener than I wish, the interview invariably turns to the matter of money. No one seems remotely interested in the effect of the Hardy Boys on the kids who read them, or how and when the books were written, or the circumstances which brought them into being. No one is ever interested in the fact that I have written hundreds of short stories, dozens of radio plays and seventy television plays, some of which were really very good.

The interest lies wholly in the fact that publishers and the Syndicate made a great deal of money out of books that have sold in the high millions, for which I was paid about $5,000.

I always realize that the interviewer feels I should be regarded as an object of sympathy or contempt—sympathy as a victim of one of the great swindles of modern times, contempt as the dumbest sucker of the age. This maddens me. It also saddens me.

I was not swindled. I accepted the terms of Edward Stratemeyer and the importance of the money was related to my needs. I was free to reject any of the assignments.

Writing is not a profession on which one embarks under duress. No one forces anyone to become a writer. No one even asks him. He writes because he enjoys writing, and if he doesn't enjoy it he should get out of the profession. It follows, then, that if he is doing something he enjoys he should not complain if the financial rewards are less than he expected or thinks he deserves.

As for the writing of books for boys, that fine writer Frank Norris explained a long time ago: "There is more significance as to the ultimate excellence of American letters in the sight of the messenger boy devouring his *Old Sleuths* and *Deadwood Dicks* and *Boy Detectives* with an earnest, serious absorption, than in the spectacle of a reading circle of dilettanti coquetting with Verlaine and pretending that they understand."

One day in the Sixties a feature writer from the *Toronto Star* came out to the small town of Whitby asking for an interview. I had written some television plays that had won a national award (the *Liberty Magazine* award for best television playwright of the year, a sort of Canadian Oscar). When he saw the old copies of the Hardy Boys in their bookcase, he asked questions.

I told him I preferred to discuss the survival problems of the freelance writer in Canada, the dexterity and versatility demanded in adapting to the new areas of storytelling with the virtual disappearance of fiction magazines. He listened politely enough and then got back to the books. How many copies had been sold? I hadn't the faintest idea.

The next day he phoned. The resourceful chap had simply called the Stratemeyer office in East Orange and talked to Harriet Adams. She told him the books I had ghosted had sold more than twelve million copies and that they were indeed the best-selling boys' books on earth. And then, of course, the film rights had been acquired by Disney, there were plans on foot for a filmed television series and the Hardy Boys comic books were doing well. The Hardy Boys Game was pretty popular too. This apparently consisted of a board marked off into sections, and you went looking for clues which would send you to the Old Mill, the Tower Mansion and other points of historic interest in Bayport. With luck you arrived safely home and collected a big reward. Otherwise, I gathered, you could find yourself adrift on Barmet Bay in a leaky rowboat.

When the interview was published the television award was mentioned in an absentminded sort of way, but the Hardy Boys held center stage. The books were now retailing at $1.25 a copy. Obviously, twelve million copies meant fifteen million dollars. Big Money! There is nothing like an association, however remote, with fifteen million dollars to elevate even a ghost to respectability.

Some time ago someone sent along a clipping from the *New York Times*. It was an interview with Harriet Adams, "daughter of Edward Stratemeyer and mastermind of several mystery adventure series that have been thrilling and chilling children for years: Nancy Drew, the Bobbsey Twins, the Hardy Boys, Tom Swift, the Rover Boys and the Dana Girls, written under assorted male and female pseudonyms." Apparently the Bobbsey Twins eclipsed every series on the list with fifty million copies. But then, they had a head start when Edward Stratemeyer invented them in 1906. Nancy Drew was next in line with thirty million copies, but the Hardy Boys were closing in fast on the inside with twenty-six million. Current annual sales showed the Bobbsey Twins dropping far behind with a quarter of a million a year. Nancy still held the lead with a million and a half a year. The Hardy Boys still held their own with an annual million.

The story added that Mrs. Adams drove to the Stratemeyer Syndicate office every day to supervise the work of eleven employees and to dictate three chapters of a book before five p.m., that she had turned out about a hundred books on her own, while providing outlines for four ghost writers. The books had been translated into seventeen languages. There was a note at the end. The staff, said Mrs. Adams, was also kept busy updating old series books.

This intrigued me enough to drop into a bookstore, pick a copy of *The Tower Treasure* from the formidable shelf — fifty Hardy Boys volumes now — and open it up. There was a neat message, in italics, on the page facing the Table of Contents.

In this new story, based on the original of the same title, Mr. Dixon has incorporated the most up-to-date methods used by police and private detectives.

It figured. I recalled a *New Yorker* article of a few years back telling how the Tom Swift series had been rewritten to bring them up-to-date in terms of modern inventions. It seemed that modern kids had found Tom and his electric velocipede a little dated.

I skimmed through a few pages of the contemporary *Tower Treasure*. It was shorter than the original, but Hurd Applegate and Adelia were still there. So was Chet Morton. I noticed that the word "roadster" had been changed to convertible. I read merely enough to suggest that the book had been streamlined, which was all right with me. After all, it wasn't my property. If the Syndicate wanted to speed it up a little and get rid of a few old-fashioned references, that was their business. I put the book back on the shelf.

Then a young man named Bob Stall, staff writer for *Weekend Magazine*, asked for an interview.

"Forget it," I said. "You'll want to talk about the Hardy Boys."

"Of course."

"But I don't want to talk about the Hardy Boys. It's all in the past."

"For you, maybe. But millions of boys *love* the Hardys. Right now. Today."

"That's fine. But I haven't written one in twenty-five years. I've written other books, I've done films, I've done a lot of television. If you want to talk about what's going on now, come along. But I would just as soon forget the Hardys."

He came anyway, with a stack of books under his arm. He didn't want to talk about films and television. He still wanted to talk about the Hardy Boys. "Look," he said, "do you realize this is a great honor for me? Talking to you, I mean."

"Come on. I don't like to be conned."

"I mean it," he said, earnestly. "You hooked me on reading. Isn't that something? Franklin W. Dixon was the first author's name I ever thought about. A living author. The rest of them were all dead. I read all the Hardy books when I was a kid and loved them. I'd have given anything to meet Franklin W. Dixon."

"And now you find there isn't any Franklin W. Dixon. He doesn't exist."

"No, he doesn't exist. He never has existed. But he always will. And when I was growing up, he lived for *me* and I used to wonder what he looked like. Thought he was probably a lot like Fenton Hardy: tall, athletic, pipe-smoking, brilliant.... "

"Disappointing, huh? Although I do smoke a pipe."

"Tell me something. What's your reaction to the rewrites?"

"No reaction at all. I know the books have been streamlined. Speeded up a little. A few cuts here and there, I suppose.

They're essentially the same books."

"You haven't read them?"

"No way."

"But they *aren't* the same books. They've been gutted. Not just revised. Completely rewritten. Changed. Don't you know?"

I shook my head. He opened the package of books. Some were old; some were new. He handed over a copy of *The House on the Cliff*. It had no dust jacket and the familiar tan cover was smudged, faded by time.

"Remember that one?"

"Look," I said, "if you're going to ask me what happened, don't bother. I can't remember what happened in any of them."

"That was the book that introduced Aunt Gertrude. It's my own copy. I've saved it for years. Read."

The book almost fell open by itself at the remembered passage. Aunt Gertrude arriving by taxi at the Hardy home. Aunt Gertrude yelling for the boys to come carry her baggage. Aunt Gertrude clinging to the yellow cat, Lavinia. Aunt Gertrude bawling out the taxi driver. Aunt Gertrude bawling out Frank and Joe....

"Yes, I remember it now," I said.

"I should think you would. What a character!" He handed over the brand-new copy of *The House on the Cliff*, the updated and abridged version. "Now look for Aunt Gertrude."

I turned the pages. This wasn't merely a streamlined version of the other. It was a different book from beginning to end. As for Aunt Gertrude, she didn't make her stormy entrance at all. I read more carefully. Aunt Gertrude didn't arrive at the Hardy home by taxi or on foot or in any other fashion. She was just *there*, and that was all. "Well I'll be damned," I said. "That was a pretty good passage. They've cut it out entirely."

"I've compared all my original copies, the ones I read when I was a kid, with all the new ones. They haven't just been streamlined. They've been gutted from beginning to end. Those old books were well written. They had words you could roll around in your mouth and taste. They had funny scenes. They had scenes you could wallow in. These new ones move faster, all right, but too fast. There's never a place to stop and linger. That's why the old ones were so great for a kid. They had flavor. And now the flavor is all gone."

Stall seemed pretty agitated by the whole thing. I looked through some of the other books, comparing the old with the new. He was right.

"The old books were written for a literate generation," said Stall. "But not these new ones. And they'll engender an even less literate generation. That's why I feel so damn strongly about it."

"The books are their property, Bob. Titles, characters, the author's name, plots—the works. They have a legal right to do whatever they wish with them."

"So what? They are using the reputation of a séries that was enormously popular because it was better written. Fathers are buying the books for their kids because they loved them when they were young. They don't know they're not the same books. They don't know that these crappy books under the same old titles with the same author's name aren't the Hardy Boys they remember."

I turned the pages again. Gone was the leisurely style. Gone were the roadsters in which the Hardy Boys drove up and down the Shore Road. Maybe Snackley and Jackley were gone too. Gone was the humor, such as it was. Even Aunt Gertrude didn't bawl out the kids any more. Aunt Gertrude— God save us all! — was playing it straight.

The world had changed for the Hardy Boys as it had changed for everyone else. It was a very strange world indeed, when a ghost could be dispossessed by another ghost. There were fifty-three titles now, even a *Handbook* in which Franklin W. Dixon instructed young readers in fingerprinting and other essentials of the detective's craft. And I had nothing to do with any of them.

I had a sense of disinheritance.

"Doesn't it upset you?" asked Stall.

"Damn it all, " I said, "what do you think? Even a ghost has feelings like anyone else."

"Can't I make it stronger than that? Let me quote you as saying the things I've just said."

"No way," I told him. "But maybe I'll quote *you*."